P9-EKH-199

The
Chinese Way
to Wealth *and*
Prosperity

The
Chinese Way
to Wealth *and*
Prosperity

8 TIMELESS STRATEGIES FOR ACHIEVING
FINANCIAL SUCCESS

MICHAEL JUSTIN LEE

NEW YORK   CHICAGO   SAN FRANCISCO
LISBON   LONDON   MADRID   MEXICO CITY   MILAN
NEW DELHI   SAN JUAN   SEOUL   SINGAPORE
SYDNEY   TORONTO

1 2 3 4 5 6 7 8 9 10   DOC/DOC   1 8 7 6 5 4 3 2

ISBN   978-0-07-178872-4
MHID   0-07-178872-7

e-ISBN   978-0-07-178873-1
e-MHID   0-07-178873-5

This publication is designed to provide accurate and authoritative information in regard to the subject matter covered. It is sold with the understanding that neither the author nor the publisher is engaged in rendering legal, accounting, securities trading, or other professional services. If legal advice or other expert assistance is required, the services of a competent professional person should be sought.

—From a Declaration of Principles Jointly Adopted by a Committee of the American Bar Association and a Committee of Publishers and Associations

Library of Congress Cataloging-in-Publication Data
Lee, Michael Justin.
    The Chinese way to wealth and prosperity : 8 timeless strategies for achieving financial success / by Michael Justin Lee.
      p. cm.
      Includes index.
      ISBN-13: 978-0-07-178872-4 (alk. paper)
      ISBN-10: 0-07-178872-7 (alk. paper)
   1. Finance, Personal. 2. Wealth. 3. Wealth—China. 4. Philosophy, Chinese. I. Title.
      HG179.L4222 2012
      332.024--dc23

                                                                                    2012017096

CONTENTS

ACKNOWLEDGMENTS

My first thanks are to God for blessing us with the freedoms and prosperity that we enjoy in the United States of America. Every day should be Thanksgiving Day in America.

Additionally, I wish to express my gratitude and appreciation to all the following:

My mother and father, Shui-Yung and Yu-Woon Lee, who in word and deed taught me everything I convey in this book.

My wife, Daphne, for unstinting support through the best of times and the worst of times.

My nieces, Talia and Ilana, and my nephews, Ethan, Asher, and Lucas, for being the wonderful grandchildren my parents always wanted.

My sisters, Hannah and Judy, for being appropriately good cop or bad cop as the occasion warranted and who in our youth put up with more from me than I care to remember.

Eyal Barzel, M.D., healer extraordinaire and the most compassionate person I've ever known.

Eric Tyson, who taught me the seminal importance of finding one's own way in writing and in vocation.

My agent, Matthew Carnicelli, for seeing the potential in this book when at first I questioned it myself.

My magnificent team at McGraw-Hill: Jennifer Ashkenazy, senior acquisition editor; Janice Race, senior editing supervisor; Lydia Rinaldi, director of publicity; Sara Hendricksen, marketing manager; and, Ty Nowicki, cover designer. No champion boxer ever had a team in his corner as wise as mine was. My most humble and respectful thanks to you all for your professionalism.

Judy Duguid, for her superb copyediting.

Leah Odom, whose charming enthusiasm for this project warmed my heart repeatedly.

Gisele Sizto, Jennifer Jiang, Bin Chen, Xiaofeng Chen, and Pen Hen Hu for your wise counsel about the sword of prosperity.

Eddie Van Halen, whose guitar pyrotechnics provided the octane to propel me through many a long night and early morning of writing.

The Authors Guild and the American Society of Journalists and Authors for their great work in defending intellectual property rights.

Finally and most important, to my precious children, Jessica and Justin, the lights of my life, who gave me the love that kept me going through a season of turmoil. You are gifts from God. I hope you will always benefit from the lessons contained herein.

With all the talk and attention paid to the rapidly growing Chinese economy and the fact that it holds a sizeable amount of the U.S. government debt, you would think more Americans would know about China, its economy, and the ways of its people. Nevertheless, we don't . . . yet we should.

Whether you want to make the most of your career, make the most of the money that you earn, or make better use of the educational system, you will benefit from reading and thinking about the lessons and stories in this excellent book.

You don't have to agree with the "Chinese" approach at all or even in part. The United States is a great and exceptional country, but China is an emerging economic force from which we can learn some things.

In *The Chinese Way to Wealth and Prosperity*, economist and author Michael Lee explains eight lessons pertaining to the enduring resilience of the Chinese people. Michael is the ideal person to write this book because he was born in Hong Kong and raised in New York City's Chinatown.

Michael has an extensive and impressive background working in the private sector as an educator, and he spent nearly two decades as an investment manager and corporate finance officer for Fortune 500 companies.

Michael has taught on the faculty of finance at the University of Maryland, Johns Hopkins University, American University, and Loyola University of Maryland, as well as on the faculty of international business at Georgetown University's Edmund A. Walsh School of Foreign Service. He served as the nation's first Financial Markets Expert-in-Residence in the U.S. Department of Labor.

In addition to tapping his own wealth of experiences, Michael cites a number of experts and presents many compelling and memorable anecdotes. He is a talented and intuitive teacher. This book will change the way you think about the Chinese, the way you think about your role in the increasingly global economy, the way you think about the opportunities the financial markets present, and the way you think about making the most of your money. Read it, enjoy it, and profit from it!

—ERIC TYSON
syndicated columnist and bestselling author,
www.erictyson.com

The
Chinese Way
to Wealth *and*
Prosperity

ACRES OF DIAMONDS

Let China sleep, for when she wakes,
she will shake the world.
—NAPOLEON BONAPARTE

I find it very remarkable given China's insular nature for so many millennia that Napoleon would have an opinion about China at all. Over the course of his storied life, he never ventured into China personally but somehow managed to express an insight extraordinarily prescient and curiously fearful for someone who feared no army. Napoleon never elaborated on why he felt this way about China, but in more recent years, many people in the business and political worlds have come to feel as he did.

In the two centuries since Napoleon's death, the rest of the world would get to know the Chinese people far better than he could have. Especially since China embarked on its ambitious capitalist experiment in the late 1970s, much attention has been paid to China and matters Chinese by economists, political scientists, sociologists, and even gourmets. I would guess that by now China has been dissected, sliced, diced, and filleted from every possible academic angle.

This attention has been for very good reason. Even through the global economic crisis, the Chinese economy has remained resilient. I contend that this resilience is a trait that is reflected in the Chinese people themselves over the centuries. Now in America, even as businesses reckon with the burgeoning clout of China, there is a growing tide of tension from the political classes. It's a fascinating situation. At the same time that businesses salivate for an expansion of ties with China, many politicians seem hesitant for the same.

I can't help feeling that there's an aura of envy in the air. But try as politicians might, they cannot turn the tides of history. And those tides have now carried China onto the global stage. As was the case with Japan in 1964 and South Korea in 1988, China's hosting of the Olympic Games in 2008 marked an unofficial and belated but conspicuous debut.

China's success has been more than mirrored by the success of the Chinese people themselves. In America, it's become cliché to apply the term *model minority* to Chinese American students (it's also applied to students with other Asian ancestries). Ask anyone who has any familiarity with high school and college campuses, and I'd wager you'd get a very similar opinion about these students. I believe that the overwhelming opinion would hold that due to a combination of familial relationships, a focus on education, and a diligent work ethic, the members of the worldwide Chinese diaspora have achieved a remarkable degree of success.

I believe these factors are correct, but I also believe they are inadequate in explaining the Chinese resilience in country after country. For one thing, these factors are certainly not unique to the Chinese. For instance, I personally have yet to encounter a single other culture that does not have an abiding focus on family and hard work. However, I do believe there are other factors that help explain the success of the Chinese people.

I intentionally avoid discussion of genetic characteristics that might account, for example, for an apparent facility with numbers or equations, because even if that were verifiable, such a discussion would be of no help to anyone without that particular DNA. Instead, I have selected those characteristics that are most replicable by anyone in any country. It is my contention that by following the principles set out in this book, anyone can attain the success that the Chinese people have found under capitalism or communism, despite discrimination and oppression (even in China), all over the globe and throughout world history.

I know that I venture into well-trod territory. The question of what makes some people more prosperous than others has bedeviled economists and political theorists for centuries. I consider this question to be one of the seminal questions of the ages.

In the end, I find myself strangely persuaded by an allegory attributed to the founder of Temple University, the preacher Russell Conwell. His story involves a prosperous farmer who desires diamonds so badly that he sells everything he owns and runs off to find his fortune. After a lifetime of trying, he dies without having achieved his goal. Meanwhile, the person who purchased his house discovered a rich diamond mine on the very property that was sold. The searching man would have found his diamonds if, instead of seeking his fortune elsewhere, he had dug in his own backyard. He would have found his *Acres of Diamonds*, as Russell Conwell entitled his work.

The central point is that one need not look anywhere for opportunity or fortune other than one's own capabilities. Russell Conwell explained the moral of his story succinctly: "Your diamonds are not in far-away mountains or in distant seas; they are in your own back yard if you will but dig for them." Conwell doesn't need to beat us over the head with his allegory. The diamonds he references are our own talents and exertions, and we all have many diamonds.

To be sure, the book *Acres of Diamonds* was only an allegory. But I believe its point is valid. There are limitless possibilities with effort and human ingenuity. Decades later, economist Julian Simon would call this roaring engine of human ingenuity and innovation the ultimate resource.

Nobel laureate Gary Becker built an entire economic subdiscipline on this topic. He called it human capital. Dr. Becker defined human capital as the entire stock of skills and knowledge we use to produce economic value. His decades-long research led him to argue that it is ultimately attitudes of human behavior which control our economic destinies.

Capital is conventionally understood in economics to refer to anything that can enhance our ability to perform useful work. Money is the most easily understood form of capital, but there are limitless numbers of others. For instance, all land, every factory, even every human being fits the description. But Dr. Becker carried the practical definition one step further.

His research concluded that tangible forms of capital are not the only kind of capital. The human is indeed a form of capital, but among human beings, factors such as schooling, punctuality, diligence, and raw intelligence provide an additional form of capital. This is easy enough to accept. Consider the substantially greater value that workers who school themselves thoroughly, comport themselves with punctuality, and demonstrate true diligence on the job can produce in economic terms.

This finding seems uncontroversial to the point of being obvious, but it was not so until Dr. Becker produced his research. Behavioral characteristics clearly fit the definition of capital as something that can enhance a person's ability to perform useful work. Dr. Becker writes that these forms of human capital are particularly compelling, because unlike land or money, people cannot be separated from their knowledge, skills, health, or values in the way they can be separated from their financial and physical assets.

Therefore, employing the terminology of Dr. Becker, all individuals, no matter how impoverished, have at least one form of capital, their human capital, their innate capacity to work. It is this capital and usually no other that the Chinese carried with them to America and across the world. But it is this human capital that has constituted acres of diamonds for millions of Chinese.

In totality, I believe that the principles in this book constitute a form of human capital that the Chinese people have in particular abundance. Each is discussed in its own chapter. I believe that upon completing this book, the reader may find some of the principles obvious. This would be quite fine as long as the reader also finds them practical. In truth, I do not wish to posit principles that are counterintuitive for their own sake. That would require a burden of proof far in excess of my interest level. Instead, I focus on the principles that readers would find easy to accept and therefore feel able to implement immediately.

It is very important to note that I do *not* suggest that these principles are unique to the Chinese people. I know that most of these principles can also explain the success of other people. But my realm of interest and my personal background require me to limit my points to the people of the worldwide Chinese diaspora, making no distinction between the Chinese of China and the overseas Chinese.

It is also very important for me to mention that I have *not* been the most diligent person in the application of these principles myself. I wish that I had been. I literally shudder when I think about the mistakes and missteps I've made in violating these principles. But the passage of time has its distinct rewards, chief among them proper perspective about what I did do, did not do, and should have done in my earlier years.

My first motivation for writing this book is to inspire my own children not to forget what has worked so well for our ancestors. My hope is that they will live these principles far better than their dear old dad did.

My second motivation for writing this book is to encourage other Chinese who may not have had the chance to explore our culture. I hope that this book can be a good starting point in clarifying a few aspects of our culture.

My final motivation is to direct some attention toward Chinese culture among non-Chinese people. With the nation's attention finely attuned to China and things Chinese, I believe this is a most propitious time. I truly believe that there is nothing that prohibits any other people from employing these principles. In fact, it is my sincere hope that many will do so. Because with their success, I will know that these Chinese principles have been validated.

CHAPTER ONE

OBTAIN "KUNG FU" IN EDUCATION

In late 2010, Yale law professor Amy Chua published a seminal, controversial article in the *Wall Street Journal* entitled "Why Chinese Mothers Are Superior." In the article, Professor Chua described some rather draconian techniques that she employed to raise her children. She wrote of a regimen of no playdates, no TV, no computer games, and hours of music practice. That was just the start. For a glimpse into such macabre childrearing, the reading public sent the article into viral territory immediately, after which the spears flew at Professor Chua for her seeming cruelty. As the child of Chinese immigrant parents myself, I objected, but only to the degree to which she took her techniques. I believe she hit the nail on the head in the subtext about the importance of the educational process to Chinese parents.

Coincidentally, right around this time, a very expansive study of global testing results was published which got surprisingly little attention but ultimately is of significantly greater importance than Ms. Chua's personal treatise.

The OECD, the Organization for Economic Co-operation and Development, a major nongovernment institution based in Paris, released the latest results in its influential Programme for International Student Assessment study. This triennial study assessed the reading, science, and math skills of 15-year-olds from public schools in all 34 OECD member states, as well as in a host of other nations. The results were not encouraging for U.S. taxpayers and must have been very disappointing for the U.S. Department of Education.

That's because in these OECD rankings, the United States, the world's most economically dynamic and prosperous country by far, could rank no higher than thirty-first in the world in mathematics. This dismal showing for American mathematical skills has by now become repetitious and expected. But to me, there was a slightly surprising outcome in the science rankings, in which the United States finished twenty-third. Imagine, the powerful United States, home to the mighty MIT and Cal Tech, ranked essentially in the high minor leagues on the science scorecard.

To fully appreciate how dismal this result is requires an appreciation of the sheer scope of America's economic dominance in the world, even now. Not many people are aware that, give or take several percentage points, the American economy accounts for about a quarter of the entire world's output. That includes China's second-place finish. Now that's economic dominance! But it would be hard to square continued economic dominance with these educational results.

The immutable fact is that for a country that has reached the stage of economic development that the United States has, scientific skills are the primary driver of future development. The days when the American economy reflected Thomas Jefferson's ideal of an agrarian society are long gone. Recent statistics reveal that no more than about 5 percent of the American workforce is engaged in agriculture. So as important as agriculture is to any country (there's a bumper sticker I occasionally see that says "No Farms, No Food!" Amen!), the industry can't be counted upon to provide great gains in employment.

Also gone are the days when the smokestacks of heavy industry could provide employment for large numbers of Americans. Since the end of World War II, the sad fact is that heavy industry has ceased to be a growing employer in the United States.

However, as these industries have declined, there has been a dramatic rise in the number of new industries in the knowledge economy, a subset of the service industries. This includes older-line computer companies like IBM and Hewlett-Packard as well as newer software juggernauts like Microsoft, Google, and Facebook. What these and so many more young companies have in common is that they are grounded in the bedrock of scientific knowledge.

This primacy of scientific skills is not limited to countries as highly developed as the United States. It can be argued that especially for countries that suffered decades of stagnation under communism and sputtered in their belated attempts to industrialize, it is science and technology they turn to in order to catapult their countries into the first world. China is a clear example of this, as is Russia.

With the United States so far below the league leaders, it is imperative to examine and adopt some of what the chart toppers have achieved. The list of the top 10 countries for all subject matters was striking in its composition. The city of Shanghai took first place, while South Korea took second, Hong Kong fourth, Singapore fifth, and Japan eighth.

There is an inescapable truth. Something is clearly going right in the Far East. For the sake of our children's futures, attention must be paid to the disparity in scores between these countries and the United States—the problem must be addressed.

What might account for this tremendous difference between the achievements of a few Asian states and those of so many others, including the United States? The simplistic answer is that these countries place a greater emphasis on education. This is obviously true and yet is inadequate in explaining the issue. It leaves open the question of why education itself is emphasized to such a degree in these cultures. The answer to this question is key.

To answer it, we must turn to the greatest sage in the history of China, the great philosopher Confucius. The modern age has not diminished the relevance of the ancient values bequeathed to us by this great philosopher. Although few people today bother to study his teachings in their original form, their impact is undeniable in all the East Asian cultures. It is for this reason that the values of loyalty, relationships, ritual, and conduct are essentially identical in China, Japan, and Korea. And we see these values reflected in the educational success of countries that profess their cultural debt to the philosopher. From the OECD results, the correlation is clear that where the Confucian values remain strong, education flourishes.

THE ROOTS OF CHINESE VALUES

What exactly is Confucianism? There is some disagreement about whether or not it is a religion, but there is no question that it has combined with Taoism and Buddhism, which are unquestionably religions, to form what we know as Chinese culture. Importantly, there is nothing mystical about Confucianism. It is more moral philosophy than religion. Therefore, believers of any religion should find Confucian principles unobjectionable.

Confucius (Kong Zi) himself is sometimes called the "Teacher of 10,000 generations" for his sagacity, but his beginnings were actually quite humble. He was little more than a commoner who despaired of the corruption of an effete dynasty. But he realized earlier than most Western political theorists that the sovereign governs via the consent of the people, even in China's monarchical system. In turn, the ruler has the mandate to listen and rule justly. But when the ruler turns tyrannical, the people have an obligation to set things right back to a harmonious and peaceful social order. His establishment of two-way rules of conduct between sovereign and subjects is paralleled by similar two-way rules of conduct between parent and child, elder and younger sibling, husband and wife, and friend and friend.

As this makes clear, although not innately a religion, Confucianism is a complete moral philosophy for leading a proper life. In totality, the canon of Confucian works, which include some principles not actually written by the Great Teacher himself, ordains an entire belief system in a right and wrong way to live and provides for the governance of human relations on the earth.

Confucianism obviously isn't the only belief system in the world. The number of competing belief systems in world history must surely be staggering, but among them, Confucianism may be unique in its exclusive focus on becoming "good." In place of a deity, liturgy, or intrinsic forms of worship, there is the teaching of obtaining virtue, and only that. This is known as Confucian moral self-cultivation.

There is instructive value even in the term itself: *moral self-cultivation*. It places the focus squarely on the self, the individual's will. In placing the focus here, there is an explicit belief that we ourselves can elevate the human spirit beyond where we commence on earth. Already, we can see the beginning of the educational imperative in the Confucian-influenced cultures.

The agenda of Confucian moral self-cultivation is truly ambitious. With rules governing all principal relationships, it is nothing less than a philosophy for setting the entire world into harmonious order. The world harmony that Confucians idealize is predicated upon each of us achieving the ultimate in our callings, and that requires continual education.

Fundamentally, the philosophy teaches that social harmony can be achieved only if humans self-actualize, to use the terminology made famous by psychologist Abraham Maslow. Confucius taught that all people are raw material and possess the same potential, but the potential must be cultivated. In perfect form, the development of that potential is the corrective means to curb any tendencies to stray from ethical behavior, which is an impediment not only to personal morality but to world harmony.

The uneducated human being in raw form would be unable to fulfill his or her personal obligation, but far worse is that such a person would also be delinquent in the monumental responsibility of advancing the world commonwealth. Let us consider the enormity of this responsibility. If one has the tools to achieve something wonderful but does not use those tools to do so, isn't there something morally blameful about that person? If we can move the world into greater harmony simply by educating ourselves but abdicate that responsibility, are we not delinquent in an unforgivable way? Max Weber, who gave us *The Protestant Ethic and the Spirit of Capitalism,* would certainly have agreed.

For Confucianists, the idea of moral cultivation is not only a possibility but a critical imperative. This then is the philosophical backing behind the Chinese, Korean, and Japanese thirst for education. It is not, as is commonly thought to be, solely for its utilitarian value, although, of course, the ability to profit from one's education is no small thing either. Neither is it for the sake of erudition itself. Someone who is erudite but remains in the Confucian definition "morally deficient" is no better than someone who is uneducated. (In a similar vein, Mark Twain once said, "The man who does not read good books has no advantage over the man who can't read them.")

Now we get to the heart of the matter. The main reason why education holds the esteemed position it does in the Chinese and Confucian societies is that education provides the very and sole means of becoming fully human. Education for its own sake just doesn't cut it.

Can it be any surprise then, with the society's humanity itself at stake, that all East Asian countries and most modern-day emigrants from those countries, such as this author's parents, prize education above all? Whether they know it or not, the entire modern generation of Asians has Great Teacher Kong to thank for imparting this great principle to us.

THE GREAT AMERICAN STORY, PART 1

This is an old story, often told, that readers of a certain age will recognize and some might even identify with. It is the story of generosity and American opportunity. It is also the story of the triumph of the human spirit through adversity and one that epitomizes the Chinese will to create prosperity.

It's about America, and it's not limited to the Chinese people. Consider the inscription at the base of the Statue of Liberty: "Give me your tired, your poor, your huddled masses yearning to breathe free." With that kind invitation, from all corners of the globe, they came to America. Why did they risk everything to journey to a new land usually without speaking a word of English? Although most Chinese immigrants would have entered the country from the West Coast instead, the story is the same as for European immigrants.

Of course, we know the answer already: to seek a better life. That we've heard the expression before does not minimize the grandeur and glory of the goal. We can only imagine what hellish existence they escaped, but their stories would all be similar. They would be harrowing stories of persecution from the king, the czar, the emperor, or some other such potentate. And they would all be true.

But they heard stories about a great place in the new world. They heard stories about streets paved with gold and might even have believed them. They heard about opportunities for religious freedom and tolerance for their beliefs and their skin colors. They heard about unlimited opportunities to make a living or a fortune. And they certainly heard about the chance to obtain educations for their children.

So they ventured forth, bidding farewell to friends and loved ones whom they surely knew they'd never see again. The passage would have been frightening. Cramped, fetid sleeping quarters would provide no relief from the nauseating seesawing effect of the oceans on the ship. Unappetizing meals would be choked down, for there was nothing else to eat. Swarms of young would join together into makeshift gangs for protection against gangs of other people. Out of frustration, minor disputes would sometimes metastasize into great fights.

But after weeks on the oceans, one glorious day, they would see far off in the distance the faint image of what appeared to be a person. One passenger informs another, then another; and before long, hundreds of passengers line the side of the ship facing the image, which grows larger. They can't quite make out the precise shape of it, but they already know what it is. It is much more than the grand gift from the people of France to the United States. It is their dream of a lifetime personified in Lady Liberty.

And after arriving, these hardy souls would live where they must, in the part of New York City closest to Ellis Island, from which they just exited. This was the Lower East

Side of New York City, where life was nasty and brutish and frequently short. The foul quarters of their passenger ship were rivaled by the conditions of their tenement existence, except that this habitation would not be transient. I know the living conditions of the tenements well. I grew up there.

A small number judge the suffering to be not worth it. They reason that if they must live hellishly, they might as well live hellishly in their homeland. But the vast majority endure their existence, never questioning the wisdom of their decision but often questioning their will.

The years pass, and although the older ones may never learn English, their children do. In fact, their children learn a great deal more. They learn the arts and the sciences of the new world. They learn well enough to excel first in grammar school, then in middle school, then in high school. Then the glorious day arrives when they graduate from university and join the ranks of the educated. The parents cannot contain their joy on this day, for it is the dream that propelled them to the United States decades before. They've done it. They've achieved the American dream.

Most Chinese would not have seen the grand lady in the harbor since they entered from the opposite coast. But this path illustrates the Chinese way, and it was shared with the Jews, the Russians, the Irish, the Italians, and myriad people before them. Their common denominator, which the Chinese recognized and epitomized, is the value of education for opportunity.

THE GREAT AMERICAN STORY, PART 2

There is also a newer story and one just as inspiring. It is the story of the American dream in the information age. In this story, the people are less desperate but equally ambitious. They cannot truthfully be described as tired or poor or as huddled masses yearning to breathe free. They indeed have yearnings, but for dreams that cannot be fulfilled in their native lands.

These dreams are of a far grander scale. The dreamers do not wish merely to make a living. They wish to make a killing. These people are even more assured than previous generations that America is the land of opportunity because they already know some who've made millions there. And they wish to share in that prosperity. So they come to America too.

They are not poor; they give up profitable opportunities they have at home. For people with their abilities, those opportunities are considerable, but they are willing to abandon them for the opportunity to capitalize upon their greatest asset, their knowledge and ambition, their true human capital.

They do not travel in cramped ships but in modern airplanes, possibly in the first-class section. They land not on Ellis Island but all across the United States. After disembarking, after a short orientation, they head to the university campuses.

They are not unfamiliar with universities. Most will have attended universities previously. Some will already hold first or even second degrees. But their journey is not over. They thirst for more knowledge, and so they enroll in graduate programs, doctoral programs, law programs, and business programs. They could have obtained this knowledge back home, but they know that knowledge obtained here is more valuable.

So they master their disciplines. They drive themselves harder than they ever have because they must master a second tongue at the same time. But they finish their race.

Then they cash in. That requires the same dogged determination that they devoted to their studies, but they persevere. From whatever country they came, they learn to embrace the fruits of this country's free market. They embrace it on the trading floors of our financial institutions. They embrace it in the labs of Silicon Valley. They embrace it in the executive suites of our major corporations. But wherever they do it, they deploy the human capital they obtained in their educational pursuits. For the newer generations, this is the Chinese Way to Wealth and Prosperity.

DR. AN WANG AND KUNG FU

Oddly enough, the telling of some relatively recent business history—involving Dr. An Wang—is necessary to illustrate this chapter's point about kung fu.

The name An Wang no longer inspires the awe it once did. In a technology age dominated by names like Gates, Dell, Brin, and Zuckerberg, the name Wang seems entirely out of place or at best antiquated. Ah, the difference two decades can make in the computer industry. Only two decades ago, the name Wang was as well known in the industry as IBM.

An Wang from Shanghai was quite a prodigy from early life. With World War II raging around him, he still managed to complete and then leverage his undergraduate degree in electrical engineering into admission to Harvard's doctoral program in physics, completing it in just three years. This might have been achievement enough for anyone else, but not for him.

Three years after obtaining his doctorate, he founded his first company, Wang Laboratories, competing directly with IBM. The next three decades would see the Wang name climb up the ranks of the Fortune 500 as Dr. Wang's brainchild supplied the needs of America's incipient computer age. Overtaking IBM was not out of the question and indeed was Dr. Wang's very goal.

By the mid-1980s, the name Wang had become synonymous with word processing and even had morphed into a verb. Secretaries and assistants were required to know how to "Wang," for instance.

Again, this would have been enough for anyone else, except for Dr. Wang. And as his wealth and fame grew, so did his philanthropy. Even now, for instance, there are the Wang Theater and the Wang Center for the Performing Arts in Boston, the city's preeminent cultural venues. For a time, there was even the Wang Institute, a graduate school of engineering.

The late 1980s saw a reversal of Dr. Wang's fortunes, as first Microsoft and then IBM introduced operating systems that made word processing simple enough on PCs that a standalone piece of hardware for that purpose was no longer necessary. But Dr. Wang's name in industry circles remains revered, as reflected in his enshrinement in the National Inventor's Hall of Fame in 1988. Mercifully, Dr. Wang would not live to see his company's devolvement in the 1990s.

For earning his doctorate and for his many other achievements, An Wang was commonly called Dr. Wang. But in the Chinese tradition, there's another title that might be appropriate. That would be to call him *shifu*, a term that pushes the Chinese veneration of education to its logical conclusion.

OF KUNG FU AND SHIFUS

A man may be able to repeat all three hundred pieces in the Poetry, but if when entrusted with office he is ineffective . . . although his learning is extensive, of what use is it?
—Confucius

Some in martial arts circles believe the word *shifu* to be the equivalent of the word *sensei* in Japanese. I understand why they think this. Students of Japanese martial arts address their instructors as sensei, and students of Chinese martial arts address theirs as shifu. But there's a world of difference between the two words. *Sensei* means simply "teacher." Therefore, a part-time remedial coach of any subject can still be called sensei in Japan. But such a person would not be called shifu in China. The reason is that *shifu* refers to one who has mastered something. Almost anything would be included—art, painting, physics, engineering, and most commonly, though frequently incorrectly, kung fu.

Indeed, the terms *shifu* and *kung fu* have a syllable in common, but most people have a completely incorrect understanding of *kung fu*. They think it means Chinese martial arts. It does not. Before Jackie Chan, before Jet Li, before Jean-Claude Van Damme, there was Bruce Lee. Not yet Bruce Lee the movie star, but Bruce Lee as Kato in the short-lived 1960s TV show *The Green Hornet*. It was this younger, fey Bruce Lee who very likely introduced the term *kung fu* into the American lexicon.

I highly doubt that even the fan base of *The Green Hornet* show (such as it was for a show that was canceled after just one season) picked up on it. But Kato would occasionally respond to boss Britt Reid's vacuity with the line, "Kung Fu's kung fu," including once in the memorable crossover show with Batman and Robin.

As noted above, the term *kung fu* is not what most people think it is. And the brilliant animated movie *Kung Fu Panda* did not help in clarifying the term. People seeing this movie and other martial arts movies probably think of images such as slashing hands and kicking feet or possibly a monk (or a panda or a raccoon, for that matter) in a pseudo-meditative pose when they hear the term *kung fu*.

In actuality, kung fu is none of those things. This is fortunate, since none of those things is likely to bring one financial prosperity. In actuality, *kung fu* simply means "mastery." Some action movies have a good or bad guy called a master of kung fu. That is actually redundant. That would mean a "master of mastery."

To be linguistically correct, one does not know kung fu; one has kung fu. What most people think is kung fu is actually the martial art *wushu*, which is a choreographed dance-like competition. Viewers watching the Beijing Olympics in 2008 might have seen the wushu competition in the late-hour broadcasting of minor sports.

But there's nothing minor about the term *kung fu*. Although someone can indeed have kung fu in the martial arts, as did the Shaolin warriors, the term is far from limited to the martial arts. The veneration of a discipline or trade to its very apex creates kung fu.

Thus, a professor can be said to have kung fu at teaching. Master chefs have kung fu in the culinary arts. Art, painting, medicine, engineering—all are areas in which the highest-trained professionals are said to have kung fu, and which frankly are more revered to most Chinese than the fighting arts. (My dear departed grandmother once told me she had kung fu in washing clothes.)

In essence, with its emphasis on education and vocational excellence, the Chinese culture winds up venerating the mastery of skills to its very core. And those with the highest-ranked skill sets are titled with the honorific shifu.

It isn't just Dr. Wang's Ph.D. from Harvard that was impressive to the Chinese, although it certainly was respected. It was also his complete mastery of the computer business which earned him the very honorable honorific Shifu Wang.

Shifu Wang, it is understood, embodied the traditional values of knowledge and practice. There's a current-day parallel here. Management consultants speak ad nauseam of concept and execution. They may criticize or endorse a business's line or criticize or approve the CEO's management of the company. For most of his career, I believe Shifu Wang would have passed these consultants' evaluations quite handily.

LEARN, THEN EARN

There probably isn't any culture in the world that doesn't give at least lip service to an emphasis on education. But in regard the topic of this book, education forms the first foundational block in any Chinese community's pursuit of prosperity. Education, at anything—with the goal of achieving kung fu at it—is the aim.

That's valuable because, especially in the United States, educational achievement and income levels go hand in hand. The conclusion is clear: the higher the educational level attained, the greater the amount of income earned. This is evident in the chart presented in Table 1-1, which uses composite data for the latest year available, 2009.

The data in the table should wake up anyone considering dropping out of college—or worse, out of high school. The lifetime earnings forgone would be tremendous. Consider first the student, who completes only a high school education versus one who completes a bachelor's degree. The income difference of $26,038, or 85 percent, was already quite surprising to me. But extrapolating the numbers for a lifetime of earnings suggests the great power of educational

TABLE 1-1

	MEAN EARNINGS FOR 2009, $
Not a high school graduate	20,241
High School graduate only	30,627
Some college, no degree	32,295
Associate's degree	39,771
Bachelor's degree	56,665
Master's degree	73,738
Professional degree	127,803
Doctorate degree	103,054
Average	42,469
Source: U.S. Bureau of the Census, 2012 Statistical Abstract of the United States	

achievement. For instance, if we assume a working lifetime of 40 years, we can begin to see the true power of an additional educational degree.

Using the most simplistic and truly unrealistic assumption that earnings remain fixed for those 40 working years, we can calculate that the high school graduate would have earned $1,225,080 over the course of a working lifetime. In contrast, by completing college, the earning potential rises to $2,266,600, a difference of $1,041,520.

It doesn't end there. Those who continue onto graduate school for a master's degree have done themselves a monumental favor, not just in the knowledge obtained but in lifetime income. Instead of the $2,266,600 they would have earned with a bachelor's degree, their lifetime income now rises to $2,949,520, a further 30.13 percent increase, or in dollar terms, $682,920 over the lifetime earnings from holding a master's degree. Now we're talking real money.

But even that isn't the end of the story. Let's add a semi-realistic qualifying assumption. For instance, let us assume that incomes rise by 2 percent per year, reflecting higher costs of living. A 2 percent growth in annual costs of living would be a reasonable inflationary assumption for a long-term rate of growth in the United States. The high school graduate would wind up having earned $1.8 million, while the graduate school graduate would have earned a total of over $4.4 million—that's about $2.6 million more.

That is just the difference between the high school graduate and the holder of a master's degree. Let's compare high school graduate with the holder of a professional degree using the same 2 percent inflationary escalation. This time, the difference in total earnings over a lifetime opens up to a Grand Canyon–sized gap of more than $5.8 million.

The record is clear and the conclusions are undeniable. Education pays off. And with their culture geared to an educational mindset, the Chinese have benefited disproportionately.

THE RECORD ABOUT MAJORS

In addition to the payoff from obtaining greater amounts of education, there is a further payoff depending on what one actually studies in college. This should come as no surprise. Surely no one would expect graduates of every major to earn the same amount of money. We just saw the variation of incomes around different educational levels. There is also great variation around the salaries of college graduates. According to the *Wall Street Journal*'s most recent salary survey, there is, as Table 1-2 shows, quite a range of starting salaries. From a low of $34,900 for education graduates to a high of $63,200 for chemical engineers, the route to prosperity takes greater shape, and the Chinese fully appreciate this.

TABLE 1-2

UNDERGRADUATE MAJOR	STARTING MEDIAN SALARY, $
Accounting	46,000
Aerospace Engineering	57,700
Anthropology	36,800
Art	35,800
Business	43,000
Chemical Engineering	63,200
Civil Engineering	53,900
Communications	38,100
Computer Science	55,900
Drama	35,900
Education	34,900
Electrical Engineering	60,900
English	38,000
Finance	47,900
History	39,200
Journalism	35,600
Marketing	40,800
Psychology	35,900
Source: Wall Street Journal	

The very high starting salaries for those who can obtain degrees in electrical, chemical, and aerospace engineering seem commensurate with the amount of work they must do in college to earn those degrees. The same goes for the next in line, computer science graduates. This last major seems to hold particular attraction for Chinese students.

Using data from the Department of Labor's Bureau of Labor Statistics, Asians, including the Chinese, account for only 5 percent of U.S. workers but make up a disproportionate share of computer software engineers (29 percent), computer programmers (20 percent), and computer scientists and systems analysts (16 percent). Anyone who's spent any time on a university campus can easily verify this disproportion.

I suspect that there's something more at work than the selection of majors for the purpose of enhanced earnings (although I'm sure that's true too). In keeping with the Chinese goal of obtaining kung fu, it is the technical disciplines that provide the most concrete opportunity for such achievement.

A RETURN TO CIVIC EDUCATION

What can modern-day America import from the Chinese culture and Confucian societies? For starters, we can provide reminders to emphasize something that seems to have been forgotten in our modern education system. Beyond vocational training, beyond mathematical formulas, beyond discourses on the various liberal arts, education's role was formerly and primarily to produce moral people.

At our country's founding, our universities were indistinguishable from schools of theology. Harvard, Yale, and Princeton were all devoted to teaching the scriptures and the classics to promising future ministers. For instance, the motto of Harvard University is still *Veritas, Christo et Ecclesiae,* meaning "Truth, for Christ and the Church." Similarly, Princeton University's motto is *Dei Sub Numine Viget,* meaning "Under the Protection of God She Flourishes." Both university mottos indicate the prominence of moral training in the early days of those institutions.

The American university system and the Ivy League are indeed still shrines of higher thought, but to a lesser and lesser extent of moral discipline. Despite the proliferation of universities to a degree unknown in any other country, we still have not created an adequate institutional movement toward the creation of "good" people. Our Founding Fathers would be aghast at our squandered opportunity. Importing some concept of moral self-cultivation would be very instructive.

First and foremost would be to inculcate some aspect of "moral" education in our school systems. I do not mean the word *moral* in the traditional generic sense. Obviously, I refer to the Confucian concept of self-cultivation. This can be done at any level of education, but I believe a targeted focus at the elementary level would be best.

A return to some form of moral education can only be a good thing. And if the word *morality* disturbs anyone, we can simply substitute a word from the not so distant American past: *civics.* Civics is similar enough to morality for all practical purposes. As was taught in an earlier time in America, civic education emphasized the rights and duties of a citizen in a good society.

Commonly wrapped up in a broader course of education about American government, the civic education of the past concerned itself with the proper conduct of a person. Consider how much more valuable to our society all citizens would be if their educations would also inculcate the virtues of responsibility toward a goal beyond the self. In such a system, education would serve the vastly greater purpose than the dissemination of knowledge for our personal intellectual elevation. Wouldn't the educational process take on a larger life? Wouldn't students see greater meaning in their pursuits? Making this clear for students at younger ages would be an invaluable lesson from the Chinese culture.

AN ELEVATION OF TECHNICAL DISCIPLINES

I believe there is a subtler lesson for Americans from the Chinese pursuit of mastery in vocation. It involves a hidden jewel in the American university system which is far too often overlooked. This is the vast system of community and vocational colleges in the United States. Frequently ignored and commonly underfunded, community colleges provide a basic education in many disciplines, including technical ones, which still present a magnificent pathway to the American middle class. We simply must abandon the attitude that community colleges are for those who cannot handle the rigor of a four-year university curriculum.

Community colleges are far more than that. In the community college system, a student can obtain shifu-like skills in disciplines from the culinary arts to mechanics, from healthcare services to information technology. These are all crucial to the proper functioning of an economy.

Even in the modern economy, individuals who graduate with an associate's degree in a vocational discipline are well on their way. Using the statistics provided earlier, people with an associate's degree would earn $2.4 million over the course of a lifetime, over half a million dollars more than those with merely a high school diploma.

It is my sincere belief that America's community colleges can serve in the front lines of a concerted effort to disseminate trade and vocational education. Very hearteningly, the *Wall Street Journal* reports that the National Association of Manufacturers is leading a drive to establish standardized curricula at community colleges across the United States with the goal of preparing students to qualify for certification in industrial skills ranging from welding to cutting metal and plastics. This is absolutely wonderful.

Also wonderful is the way community colleges are starting to create custom training programs for employers, with the goal of moving toward competency-based education. Confucius would have approved of that term.

Just as he spoke of self-cultivation as a lifelong pursuit, it would be instructive to create higher and higher shifu-level certification programs for technical disciplines beyond the associate's degree. Private-sector initiatives can continue to lead here. One wonderful example created by the information age is the certification for specific technical skills. For example, Microsoft certification is a highly prized designation for systems analysts. On the nontechnical side, trade groups like the National Institute for Metalworking Skills have instituted credentials also. Both are great because they emphasize mastery.

We must continue this into every branch of the working world. Let us further professionalize and even glorify these highly critical roles in our economy, because in doing so, we can bring kung fu to all walks of work. This in turn creates prosperity.

CRITICAL CAVEAT: DON'T TAKE TOO LONG EDUCATING

The importance of obtaining a good education can't be challenged. However, I am well aware that in the United States, education can come at a very high cost. It would be beyond the scope of this book to discuss methods of financing that education. It must be admitted that the years spent pursuing higher and higher levels of education necessarily shorten the number of years that one has left to reap the benefits of that education. As we will see in Chapter 5, there is a critically powerful factor at play in the loss of earnings in those years. It is the time value of money. The calculation needed to make up for it will be explained in Chapter 5.

The road has been paved, and the hope is that the student is ready. Especially for younger readers, the task may seem daunting. But here's a simple first step. Invest in a library card. It's free. The return on any investment that is free is literally limitless. Then use it. That's it. The younger a student first obtains one, the better overall the student will be. Among his other gifts to society, Benjamin Franklin must be thanked for helping to establish the first lending library in early America. These days, the nation's libraries are full of knowledge that anyone can obtain by doing nothing more than walking into one. There is nothing that is as simple and yet that provides such immense benefits as obtaining a library card.

A CLOSING THOUGHT

Consistent with the theme of this book, this chapter focused on the financial benefits of obtaining a good education. But clearly the benefits don't stop there. Confucius would surely contend that the financial benefits of becoming educated are trivial to the point of being inconsequential. Of course, he is right in the grand scheme of things. If they could be measured, the total returns on a person's education would transcend anyone's ability to calculate. There is a satisfaction that comes from obtaining an education that no amount of money can provide.

SUMMARY

The record is clear. Education pays off. And because the Chinese culture has bequeathed a legacy for educating a person to become a grand master, the continuing Chinese heritage places more than a responsibility on education; it places an obligation on it. These obligations are to one's family, to one's community, and to the greater society at large. It is known or at least accepted in Chinese communities that education lifts the humanity of the person and by extension one's community as well.

Therefore, the first principle of the Chinese Way to Wealth and Prosperity is to obtain a fine education and then apply it.

CHAPTER TWO

GO MOBILE

In the fourteenth century, the Muslim traveler Ibn Battuta wrote about the many people he'd met on his journeys. He commented that "nowhere in the world are there to be found people richer than the Chinese." Whatever the truth of his statement, it is undeniably true that there have been few people throughout history who have been as peripatetic as the Chinese. It is therefore no great surprise that Ibn Battuta would have encountered them in his travels.

Although mass waves of Chinese emigration would only begin in earnest in the nineteenth century, there is evidence of Chinese emigration even before the birth of Christ to surprisingly distant lands. And the emigrants were quite successful.

Professors Homer Dubs and Robert Smith of Duke University have written about the success of the Chinese in Mexico as early as 1635. I can't even imagine how they crossed the ocean, but according to the professors, in a sign of tragic developments to come in later centuries, Spanish barbers were already complaining about competition from Chinese barbers. As a result, the viceroy decreed that the number of Chinese barbershops be limited to 12 and must be located in the suburbs in order to eliminate the "unfair" competition. The implicit success of the Chinese barbers in Mexico in 1635 serves as a perfect metaphor for this chapter.

AROUND THE WORLD IN TWO MILLENNIA

These first emigrants traveled for far less dire reasons than did those of the mass waves that followed. In greatest likelihood, the first Chinese emigrants were traders plying their wares as distantly as the Tigris and Euphrates Rivers. Although Ibn Battuta did indeed travel to China, it is also possible that the specific Chinese he referred to in the opening quote of this chapter were these emigrant traders.

The point remains that as early as the middle of the second millennium, the Chinese people were making their mark in commerce around the world, impressing the Mexican viceroy (negatively) and Ibn Battuta (positively).

These early traders were in the vanguard of many subsequent waves of Chinese emigration. However, in contrast to the early traders, those who left in the later mass emigrations did so primarily to escape the many wars and frequent famines in China. These later emigrants would not have been of the same pedigree as the early traders. They were primarily poorly educated peasants and manual laborers. At least at first, they would have had no choice but to perform coolie labor.

But they were of hardy stock equal to that of the traders. They had to be. They might have had fewer material possessions than the traders, but their human capital would have been great. They would bring their "acres of diamonds" with them across the oceans to Southeast Asia, Europe, Australia, South Africa, and eventually to the Americas. The dreams they had would have been identical to those of all immigrants discussed in Chapter 1. In time, with the success of the early waves making news back home, greater and greater numbers would jettison everything to venture abroad.

By the end of the twentieth century, Chinese people not living in China, commonly called *overseas Chinese*, constituted the single largest group of minority people in the world. It is estimated that currently there are over 40 million overseas Chinese in the world. For perspective, this is about the same number of people in America's six largest cities (New York City, Los Angeles, Chicago, Houston, Dallas, and Washington, D.C.) put together. It's also larger than the entire population of Argentina, Canada, or Poland. The noise made by this group would have resounding implications for those still in the home country.

A RECORD OF ACHIEVEMENT
AND BACKLASH

Unfortunately, the story about the viceroy's decree in Mexico reflected an opinion toward the Chinese that would become regrettably common. From the plantations of Southeast Asia to the gold fields of California, the overseas Chinese suffered oppression after oppression, bearing their literal scars with as much dignity as anyone could. Their sob stories would not have been unknown back home. Why would others follow?

It's even harder to understand when we note that in China's dynastic system, emigration from China was a capital crime. The emperor had decreed that anyone settling outside of China would be beheaded, thereby ensuring one-way passages only. There is only one answer to the question. It was to pursue opportunity. By itself, this is nothing unusual. Migration is hardly limited to Chinese people. What does make it unusual is that migration would continue despite the persecutions that would occur in many of the host countries.

Unusual perhaps, but actually it is not illogical. Wherever the Chinese landed, despite the traumatic stories they'd have heard, the new arrivals still sought to beat the odds and gain control of their destinies. It's the classic trade-off principle. Stay in China and accept the deprivation. Leave for a new land and risk persecution but gain the possibility of a better life. More would choose the path of less resistance. But many would accept the challenge of emigration.

Those who chose to leave needed a great spirit of enterprise and a genuine willingness to be mobile. The subsequent achievements of the Chinese in foreign lands suggest a hardiness and resilience in those who attempted the voyage. Because the penalty for failing in the new land was the ultimate one, only the hardiest (or foolhardiest) would attempt the venture. But having attempted the venture, the same indomitable spirit would carry them very far in the new land, despite brutal oppression. It's social Darwinism in a sense. This spirit of risk taking augured very well for the economic prosperity of their descendants.

AN EXCEPTIONAL EXCEPTIONALISM

Let's fast-forward to the present. The Chinese continue to migrate, but the picture is now completely different. No longer do the Chinese leave China packed like sardines in the belly of floating prisons. No longer are bloodthirsty mobs waiting to lynch them at the slightest opportunity. These Chinese newcomers are breaking through glass ceilings regularly, and tales of success are so commonplace as to sound trite.

Chinese emigration continues, primarily to the United States. But now the migration moves in both directions. The flow of people into the United States remains for both economic reasons and for educational reasons, but in the past two decades there has also been a vast movement of capital and people back to China.

This reverse migration seems likely to continue. Although the United States has undeniably been more hospitable to the overseas Chinese than ever before in history, many feel that the best days for investment in America are past. On more than one occasion, I have personally met Chinese immigrants, having completed the laborious process of obtaining U.S. citizenship, later choose to renounce it. The reason given each time was to avoid paying federal taxes that are levied on income earned by American citizens anywhere in the world.

Just on the numbers, their logic seems sound. Looking at the current size of America's debt burden, these former citizens calculate that tax rates must rise eventually to repay this debt and don't wish to remain citizens when that happens. This is especially the justification if they don't intend to stay in the United States anyway, which is true in many cases. Ultimately, the cost-benefit analysis persuades many not to bother with the U.S. passport when a Chinese one opens as many doors as they'll ever need.

There is already talk of a "Chinese exceptionalism," a play on the term coined by Alexis de Tocqueville, "American exceptionalism." American exceptionalism refers to the belief that the United States is uniquely superior to other nations. The specifics of American ideology that are exceptional are its liberty, egalitarianism, individualism, populism, and laissez-faire principles. To many Americans, including me, the United States as a "shining city on a hill" still resonates.

But it isn't the only opinion out there. I imagine that citizens of every nation subscribe to some form of national exceptionalism. What may be unique about Chinese exceptionalism is the enormous ground it has gained in its usage among non-Chinese. The global financial crisis, which many attribute to laxity in U.S. regulation, has only accelerated this trend.

The sheer magnitude of Chinese exceptionalism, however it is defined, is reflected in the amount of the country's foreign reserves, which at the time of this writing, nears $2 trillion. By any standard, that actually is truly exceptional, and the people of the world are taking notice.

EXODUS TO AMERICA

Reading Chinese history is not for the faint of heart. I often wonder how my ancestral line managed to stay intact through all the upheaval it has sustained over the millennia. The devaluation of life that the Chinese people have endured both within China and outside the country is heartbreaking in its tragedy.

Imagine you are a citizen of old China. Especially for those in the south of China, it is a brutal existence. As in most countries of the time, agriculture is the dominant form of employment, although even great effort would hardly guarantee enough to eat. The people hear talk about the great imperial exams through which people may earn their way into the bureaucracy, but there is no time to study or money to pay teachers. So they continue working the land. That is, until the brigands attack. Since southern China is far from the country's capital, protection is scarce, and calls for help are, tragically, answered too late or even ignored. Life is intolerable, and so escape is a logical alternative.

Geography would seemingly be an asset because of the proximity of the South China Sea. But however noble the attempt, the resultant reality was often the opposite. The history of the Chinese in America is a good starting point. This history was quite harrowing at times. The first Chinese arrived in America in the early 1800s seeking relief from the deprivations of China. They would have had dreams that were indistinguishable from those of generations of other immigrants. But life for many turned out quite different from what they expected.

THE CHINESE AMERICAN
EXPERIENCE, PART 1

Ultimately, this is a story of triumph over adversity. But not at first. The first wave of Chinese immigration to the United States began with the California gold rush. Attracted to the precious metal, as all people are, the Chinese sailed east to find some of their own. Work was plentiful, though hospitality was not. There is a grisly expression that seems to date back to the time of the gold rush and the building of the First Transcontinental Railroad. The expression is "a Chinaman's chance," and it means hardly any chance at all. While its derivation isn't known for sure, none of the possible explanations is pleasant. Many believe that it referred to the practice of sending a "Chinaman" down the side of a cliff or to another precarious place with dynamite in order to clear obstructions or open a passage. If the worker were not lifted back or extricated somehow else before the blast occurred, the person would perish. Hence, the phrase was coined to describe an endeavor in which someone had a negligible chance of succeeding in these risky circumstances.

And these were the good times. As the gold rush waned, the rail lines were completed, and work decreased, animosity reared its nasty head. Waves of overt violence were directed against the most different foreigners, the Chinese, giving the metaphor about a Chinaman's chance a new connotation. The "Chinaman" had only a Chinaman's chance of surviving even in the streets.

This animosity would drive the Chinese from all work until they could create encampments in cities like San Francisco and earn just enough to live on. Still, many Chinese found even such an outcast existence preferable to conditions in China. The immigration continued. Such was the continued flow of arrivals into America that by 1880 an estimated 10 percent of California's population was Chinese.

Of course, this was even more intolerable to the locals. When even violence and scare tactics could not stem the tide of immigration, the people turned to legislation. And in 1882, the despicable Chinese Exclusion Act went into effect.

THE CHINESE AMERICAN
EXPERIENCE, PART 2

It wasn't pretty, was it? But I did call it a story of triumph over adversity. Part 1 is the story of triumph over unbelievably miserable conditions resulting from the Chinese people's geographic mobility. Never mind what it means about old American attitudes, the history speaks volumes for the spirit of Chinese enterprise. The people didn't flinch in the face of an angry ocean, and they continued not to flinch in the face of an angry population or angry legislation. The Chinese settlements would first survive and then thrive.

Part 2 of the American experience for the Chinese would be considerably brighter. Although it would take 61 years, on December 17, 1943, Congress finally passed the Chinese Exclusion Repeal Act, which allowed the Chinese to enter the United States legally once again. It can't be said that the law was repealed for moral or humanitarian reasons as much as for political reasons. With the United States and China on the same side in World War II, the American government needed to keep relations strong. In the wake of this, the Chinese settlements, which had survived during the Chinese Exclusion Act, began to thrive and proliferate. Rather quickly, the original California encampments extended to adjacent towns, then to adjacent states, as did the Chinatowns from the East Coast. And our modern Chinatowns were born.

These Chinatowns would not spring up by fiat. But with the same spirit of adventure that our American frontiersmen would exhibit, Chinese entrepreneurs would create communities and even minicities out of nothing but slums. The educational drive of these entrepreneurs' children would take over from there. The rest, as they say, is history.

THE STORY IN SOUTHEAST ASIA

The record elsewhere around the world is no less harrowing but just as triumphant. Beginning in earnest in the late nineteenth century, emigration from China to neighboring countries in Asia coincided with China's decline.

Just like the Chinese immigrants to America, Chinese immigrants to Southeast Asia had no apparent advantages. They did not have any special skills. They had even less money. Many did not even have family with them. But they did have a large base of human capital. And that made all the difference.

In country after country, their story was the same. Through the powerful combination of industriousness and thrift, the Chinese communities would spring up to become wealthy within a few generations. Benjamin Franklin would have approved of their method.

Just as in California, starting with small encampments, the Chinese immigrants would create larger communities, then virtual cities. Along the way, they would establish their own schools and housing communities. Always seen as outsiders and interlopers, they were denied credit and banking resources. So they would create the equivalent of mutual aid societies. Modern-day microfinance would have been common where deals were consummated with gentlemen's agreements. From such humble beginnings, the Chinese would carve a large place for themselves in each country to which they'd trekked.

CASE STUDY 1. ROBERT KUOK

Robert Kuok of Malaysia offers a picture-perfect example of the Chinese propensity to be mobile in pursuit of success. Kuok's story is truly a rags-to-riches story.

Born in 1923 to parents originally from Fujian, China, Kuok sailed with his family across the vicious South China Sea to settle in Malaya, predecessor to modern Malaysia. Not only was his lineage humble, but so was his early working life, which seems to be typical of stories involving the overseas Chinese.

At the age of 25, Kuok founded his first company with his brothers, and his rise began. Theirs was a trading company devoted to the wholesale purchase and sale of agricultural commodities. Then, as now, this was no occupation for the timid. To make money at it, the trader must correctly anticipate movements in commodities and take large enough positions in ones expected to rise in price and realize a profit from their sale at the future higher prices. This happens to also be the modus operandi of stock trading.

Kuok had initial successes that would already make the case for his inclusion in this chapter, but for him the best was yet to come. Consistent with the principle illustrated in this chapter, he traveled to England to learn the workings of the London Commodities Exchange, then the world's largest. He must have been a diligent student, for when he returned, he knew enough about sugar operations and pricing dynamics to found Malaysia's first sugar refinery.

From this first refinery, Kuok would eventually build a sugar monopoly in his adopted homeland. Evidently not satisfied with conquering one industry, he chose to diversify into the hospitality industry by creating the Shangri-La Hotel chain. Anyone who's traveled to modern Asia would agree that Kuok's hotels live up to their storied name. Currently, Shangri-La Hotels operate all through Asia, the Middle East, and even Australia, the United Kingdom, and Russia.

Apparently still not content, Kuok would extend his financial mobility much further. Eventually, his holdings would include stakes in broadcasting, newspapers, flour milling, animal feed, oil, mining, finance, freight, and real estate.

Still not done, Kuok continued to broaden his interests. In the end, Robert Kuok's career provides a compelling example of the principle I wish to illustrate, an exceptional example to be sure, but illustrative nevertheless. Seeking opportunity, his parents left the familiarity of China for a strange land. One generation later, a member of Forbes 400 was created, one who is currently worth an estimated $14 billion. While I'm sure Robert Kuok would credit many factors for his success, one critical step was his first, his willingness to embrace mobility.

CASE STUDY 2. LIEM SIOE LIONG

Another fine example is provided by Indonesian tycoon Liem Sioe Liong. Like Robert Kuok's family, Liem Sioe Liong's family was from Fujian, China. And like Kuok, Liem would leave China to seek his fortune offshore. He chose Indonesia. Further, like Kuok, Liem would start with an agricultural commodity. In his case, it was the peanut oil business that his brothers had founded. But before long, Liem had diversified his family's holdings. His second commodity was the clove market, cloves being a major ingredient in the cigarettes favored by the locals. This early success would already have vindicated his emigration from China. But just like Kuok, his best was yet to come.

A watershed moment came during the revolution when the Indonesians overthrew the Dutch colonialists. Not one to miss an opportunity and eager to prove his patriotism, Liem provided Indonesian soldiers with medical supplies. In the aftermath of the bloody revolution, his businesses absorbed many of the former Dutch assets.

The defeat of the Dutch overseers was not ordained, and Liem took immeasurable business and personal risks by backing the Indonesians. But like any business endeavor, it was the risk he took that would create immense rewards later.

After moving to the capital city of Jakarta in 1952, he expanded his connections substantially with other Chinese businesspeople in the region. Eventually, his empire included major holdings in soap, textiles, flour, and banking. But he was still not done. With Indonesia's industrialization just beginning, he realized that the need for core building materials would grow at a rapid pace, particularly cement. Thus, he undertook another big challenge, to conquer the nascent Indonesian cement industry. He succeeded with Indocement, which remains one of the world's largest cement companies. His successes continued to pile up until his net worth approached $1 billion. As with Robert Kuok, many factors led to his success, but one thing is clear. The fortune that he made in Indonesia could not have been made if he'd stayed in China during these years.

CASE STUDY 3. ELAINE CHAO

Our final case study illustrating the Chinese propensity to travel for opportunity is provided by the former U.S. Secretary of Labor, Elaine Chao. Born in Taiwan, she immigrated with her family to the United States at the age of eight. This success story actually has two protagonists, Secretary Chao and her father, Dr. James Chao.

It was Dr. Chao who came first to the United States. Despite his medical degree, he sought more; his goal was to establish himself in the shipping industry, which he did. And, in fact, he became quite successful with his company, Foremost Shipping Company, which conducted increasing amounts of trade with China. His success by itself is enough to make my point, but it is his daughter who truly shines as an avatar of geographic and upward mobility.

Dr. Chao brought his daughter Elaine over for her education. After completing her MBA at Harvard Business

School, Elaine Chao became chairperson of the Federal Maritime Commission, and after that, director of the Peace Corps. Following this, she was named president and chief executive officer of United Way of America.

But the high point of her career came later when President George W. Bush nominated her to be U.S. Secretary of Labor in 2001. She went on to serve the American people faithfully for eight years, the only member of President Bush's cabinet to do so. In her tenure, she was the first Asian American woman and first Chinese American in the history of America to be appointed to a president's cabinet.

The daughter of a physician anywhere in the world would unlikely to be living a life of deprivation, but the number of opportunities available in Taiwan could not match the sea of opportunities she would find in the United States. She doesn't seem done yet, but what she's accomplished thus far already establishes her as a veritable model of the second principle of the Chinese Way to Wealth and Prosperity.

These case studies of three admittedly exceptional individuals nevertheless provide valuable lessons for the rest of us. I believe two are particularly critical.

LESSON 1. BE WILLING TO UPROOT AND REROOT

Mobility is absolutely crucial in the modern labor market. To navigate through the cruel vicissitudes of the modern employment market, the labor force must always be seeking out opportunities beyond its own backyard. If job security ever actually existed, it certainly does not now, which makes this principle particularly critical.

At the time of this writing, the economy is weak and may remain that way for years. But even if it doesn't, there can be no denying that a new mindset must be adopted. Gone are the days when careers can be local or even provincial. The term *globalization* is quite trite, but in this case, it's become trite from accurate usage. The world's opportunities have indeed gone global, and the labor force must adjust to them.

For instance, on the strength of China's breakneck economic growth of the past two decades, many jobs have been created in China, and some will beckon to foreigners to provide expertise that does not exist in China. This cannot continue forever, but for now it appears that even as capital investment flows into China, so do some employment opportunities. This is the very reason for the reverse migration to China in recent years.

One needn't be Chinese to capitalize upon this. Nor is this phenomenon limited to China. The same story can be told for many of the emerging countries in the world. Opportunities may not abound, but they always exist for the adventurous and the willing.

It must be said that not everyone of the older generation has the appetite to venture abroad. That's accepted. But those of the younger generation have no excuse. In the reverse direction of the Chinese emigrants of generations past, the younger generation must seek out and embrace these opportunities far from their own backyard. But they needn't worry. Their acres of diamonds will travel with them as surely as the Chinese emigrants' did when they crossed the ocean in the opposite direction. These diamonds will provide as much job security as can exist in the modern working world.

LESSON 2. INVEST BEYOND YOUR BACKYARD

Those who can no longer venture abroad personally still have their chance to profit from vicarious mobility. It's in the area of their personal finances.

There was a time, not so very long ago, when an American's stock portfolio could consist entirely of U.S. stocks. It seemed to make enough sense. After all, if one has always lived in America, still lives in America, and expects to always live in America, doesn't it make sense to invest entirely in America? Actually, the answer is no.

The reason is not just that emerging countries are expected to have higher investment returns. That point is usually conceded, but it only stands to reason that higher investment returns must be accompanied by higher levels of risk. And that might be unacceptable to many people.

Luckily there's a meeting point. Those who've studied finance at the university level will be familiar with the work of William Sharpe, Nobel laureate in economics in 1990. This chapter cannot do justice to his work, but we can still use his basic principles for our purposes.

Dr. Sharpe proposes that any collection of stocks has a definable risk. Since stocks always rise and fall to different degrees, any subset of them will have a different risk from any of them individually. That subset of stocks is a mixing bowl of their individual risks. By combining them, we get a resultant portfolio that has a lower risk than any of the stocks individually have. Sound too good to be true? It isn't. It is simply the principle of diversification.

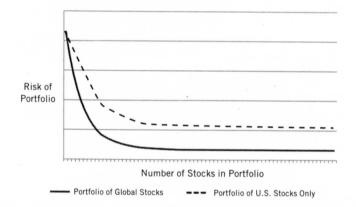

Number of Stocks in Portfolio

────── Portfolio of Global Stocks　　▬ ▬ ▬ Portfolio of U.S. Stocks Only

We can see the end result in the graph above. In normal times and in most cases, as we increase the number of stocks in a portfolio, we will reduce the risk of the overall portfolio down to some limit. But if we do not confine our investment to U.S. stocks, the risk reduction is even greater. It is no wonder that the talking heads on the business news channels so frequently discuss non-American stocks. It only stands to reason that such stocks offer the greatest potential benefit to the American investor in terms of risk reduction.

Just as younger workers must consider moving beyond their comfort zones to obtain ideal employment, so must the rest of us consider deploying our money beyond our comfort zones to obtain ideal investment returns. In so doing, the investor would be demonstrating a modicum of the hardiness that immigrants all over the world exhibited in uprooting their entire lives. It's asking very little.

SUMMARY

Economist and sociologist Thomas Sowell of the Hoover Institution has written extensively about the characteristics of migrant peoples. He brilliantly points out that people who have the stomach to leave their homeland in the first place, leaving everything behind, very likely have the stuff that converts big dreams to reality.

It's a Darwinian process that skews the distribution of the successful toward the immigrant. This process isn't limited to the Chinese, but it practically defines the Chinese immigrant experience.

Therefore, the second principle of the Chinese Way to Wealth and Prosperity is to get mobile and go global in pursuit of opportunity.

CHAPTER THREE

UNDERSTAND THE VALUE OF GUANXI

Has there ever been a phenomenon like Facebook? With all due credit to Apple, Microsoft, Google, and Amazon, the revolution that is Facebook has set the bar higher than it has ever been set before by a technology company. If Facebook were a high school student, it would surely get voted most popular in its graduating class as well as in all previous graduating classes.

Even mighty Microsoft needed 10 years to gain its first grand foothold. In contrast, Facebook, founded only in February 2004, already had more than 600 million users by early 2011. Now that's rapid growth.

Such has been its clout that the protestors who participated in the popular uprisings in Egypt that toppled President Hosni Mubarak publicly thanked Facebook for being the logistical platform that they used to communicate their movements. Was this even conceivable just a few years ago? Consider the enormity of a phenomenon launched out of a dormitory room that would be strong enough to disrupt an entrenched political order in an authoritarian regime. It boggles the imagination.

With such global acceptance, it should come as no surprise that Facebook's founder, Mark Zuckerberg, became very rich, very young. With precise valuations not immediately available, *Forbes* estimates Zuckerberg's worth at an astounding $13 billion. The jaws of the world drop.

To his considerable credit, Zuckerberg homed in on one underlying philosophy that had already been universally accepted, and then he managed to deliver it technologically. That philosophy is the connection of social beings to one another. The critical importance of such connection forms the third principle in the Chinese way to wealth.

CONNECTING SOCIAL BEINGS

The importance placed on the family unit is a well-known characteristic of Chinese culture. But that's certainly not unique to the Chinese. I'm sure every culture values closeness and connectedness in its families. However, what is unique is how the Chinese have added an additional dimension to their family connectedness. In so doing, an additional aspect of human capital is created among Chinese people.

There is a Chinese term, *guanxi* (pronounced approximately as "gwan-shee"), which is becoming known in global business circles. Some have translated this word as "network." That's not entirely off base, but it actually goes further than that. As it is conventionally understood, business networking involves the search for like-minded people to create or enhance business activity. The rise of the Internet has certainly accelerated possibilities for conventional business networking.

In contrast, guanxi refers to a system of personal relationships that are bonded together by the reciprocal exchange of favors. This differs dramatically from conventional business networking, which may indeed have a give-and-take element but does not rely on it. For example, business networks on Facebook, which has a special interest group for nearly everything under the sun, provide instant acceptance for a vast segment of the population. This is wonderful, but the very ease of entry into and exit out of these groups limits its comparison to guanxi.

Creating guanxi is not easy. It could involve years of cultivation just to find the right counterparty and opportunity for which to perform and then request a favor. Meanwhile, the counterparty is doing his or her own calculation. What both parties are calculating is their potential gains. If the deal is amenable, a favor is done. And once the favor is done, the bond is permanent—it survives long after the reciprocal favor is done. Forever more, both parties have a higher level of trust and camaraderie established by this back and forth, and so the favors can continue indefinitely. Over time, the finest guanxi relationships can even approximate familial bonds in their tightness.

FAVORS AND OBLIGATIONS

The same Confucian culture that gave the Chinese their hearty appetite for education gets some credit here too. Without actually stating the principles of guanxi, it was nevertheless Confucianism that clarified the primary tenets of relationships in a properly functioning society. This is important, because an understanding of relational issues is key to successful guanxi.

The five key relationships that are crucial in Confucian study are between (1) ruler and subject, (2) parent and child, (3) elder sibling and younger sibling, (4) husband and wife, and (5) friend and friend. The Confucian ordering of society along relational lines gives a sense of how guanxi may have arisen. The five primary relationships are explicitly defined. However, guanxi works by creating relationships where none are explicitly defined by the Confucian code. Thus, where no clear relationship exists, the Chinese people augment the "stranger" dynamic with the creation of a bond.

This transcends the Confucian friend-to-friend relationship. In guanxi relationships, the participants need not actually like each other. Indeed, they might even despise each other. But that's not of primary importance because, like the sibling relationship, the bond of guanxi creates obligations that transcend personal likability.

Again, the starting thread of a guanxi bond is a favor. The favor could be as minimal as a kind word on someone's behalf or as grand as the hiring of a new CEO. In any case, after the favor is done, an obligation is created that has no expiry. It would not be unusual for a favor to be "repaid" toward the end of one's life or for the repayment to extend to one's family after one's life has ended. But an accounting of the favor is never forgotten.

This understanding of favor and obligation is what so critically distinguishes Chinese guanxi from normal business networking. I realize that to Western ears, this may seem crass or even extortionate. After all, in the Judeo-Christian ethic, favors performed are seen as acts of charity. It would be very unseemly for the one performing the favor even to mention it, let alone expect repayment for it. Not so in Chinese culture. Favoritism in the neutral, generic sense of the word is rather par for the course, and not just in business. It is as natural as the repayment of a bank loan. Although the obligation to reciprocate a favor does not appear as a liability on anyone's accounting statement, it is little different from that. It is simply the future cost incurred for the benefit received in the present.

This point deserves emphasis. Favoritism and nepotism are not seen in the same negative light in Chinese culture as they are in Western society. Both are expected. Especially in olden days, it would not have been unusual for authority figures to draw extensively from their guanxi web to fill employment vacancies. This might seemingly prevent the most suitably qualified person from being employed for the position, but from the Chinese perspective that would be considered a micro cost of maintaining the greater macro benefit of the continuation of the guanxi network. It would simply be taken at face value that the fulfillment of a vacancy requires a guanxi connection. This lesson is still being learned by American businesses seeking entry to the Chinese market.

The universal acceptance of these unofficial "off-balance-sheet" accounts explains why personal affection is not necessarily part of the equation. Trust, however, is. One who owes must be trusted to repay. The more favors that are performed, the more reciprocal obligations that are created. In society as well as in business, any party's obligation to repay is built into the planning for eventualities, much like the management of a modern-day supply chain. And like a modern-day supply chain, it only works if every interconnected part can be counted on to serve its role. The old saying about a chain being only as strong as its weakest link applies very much in guanxi.

As can be expected, since trust in reciprocity is the key factor in maintaining the guanxi web, failure to reciprocate is an unforgivable offense. The loss of face would be tremendous and irrecoverable. Total ostracism is likely.

Traditionally, when two Chinese people meet for the first time, it doesn't take long before the conversation turns toward an exploration of each other's guanxi connections. This exercise allows both people to place themselves within a wider context. There might not be any connection, but if not, then like a shrewd salesperson, the more skilled guanxi operators would attempt to instantly build one. At its highest level, skilled guanxi operators will create entire careers around building and utilizing their guanxi web.

The most skilled of these operate much like Don Corleone from Mario Puzo's *The Godfather*. One turns to the Godfather for the favor of assistance, connection, retribution, or less commonly, money. Just as depicted in the movie, it is understood afterward that Don Corleone may call upon the person, though that time may never come, to do something in return. This is a reasonable depiction of a guanxi transaction in creation.

Another example comes from James Clavell's wonderful novel about intrigue and machination in Hong Kong society, *Noble House*, which fictitiously but fairly depicts the role of favors and the extent to which obligated parties must go to fulfill those obligations. In that classic telling, the story practically turns on the fulfillment of an obligation from long ago.

THE OVERSEAS DIASPORA

The historic value of the guanxi network can be seen in how the Chinese have operated outside China. The story of Chinese migration has already been recounted in Chapter 2. That's one facet of Chinese human capital. A corollary employs what the Chinese needed to survive after their sojourn had ended.

Consider the lonely Chinese immigrant. Whether to Thailand or Malaysia or Indonesia or even the United States, the immigrants arrive with next to nothing. While some destinations may be less hostile than others, a warm welcome could not realistically be expected. So what do they do? They gather in groups. These gatherings will eventually form Chinatowns, but at first they are no more than groups of loose acquaintances.

But that's enough to start a guanxi web. Let's say person A knows that person B requires something that person C wishes to sell. Person A now has the opportunity to broker a transaction. If the transaction completes, both B and C have an obligation to A. (B and C, having engaged in a mutually acceptable transaction, do not owe each other anything.)

Now let's say, as time goes by, A has a cousin coming to America but is having some paperwork difficulty back home, a difficulty that B can remedy. What's the easiest solution? Surely it is not to complain to the government authorities. Rather, it would be to call upon B to fulfill the obligation entered into years ago and come up with a solution. Effective? Definitely.

Even the sale of guanxi obligations is common. If person A knows that he or she will never need what person B can supply, person A can consider selling person B's obligation, like a share of stock, to person D. Person D, in turn, can sell it to person E. And it can continue down the line in this manner until, eventually, person B may be obligated to someone many times removed from the original person owed the favor. This is normal. Thus, the Chinese immigrant who may not have any financial capital upon arrival may actually have even more valuable capital in the form of obligations that must be fulfilled. This is infinitely more precious than a generic letter of introduction. It's practically an invitation to join a family.

It must be said that the modern age has certainly eroded the gentleman's agreement aspect of traditional guanxi favoritism. I must assume that any modern businessperson would hesitate to perform a big favor without lawyers being present to contract for the reciprocal obligation. But this doesn't completely nullify the importance or the value of guanxi's quid pro quo. Even in the modern era, the ability to cultivate guanxi is the most distinguishing characteristic between those who succeed in China and those who don't.

The record is clear: for the foreign businessperson wanting to do business in China, there is no substitute for guanxi. Don't leave home without it.

CLANS AND MICROFINANCE

In Catholic social teaching, there is a concept known as *subsidiarity*. Very generally, this principle articulates a hierarchy for organizational efficiency. Tasks ought to be handled by the smallest, lowest, or least centralized competent authority. For instance, if there is a family dispute, it should not be elevated to any higher level for resolution. What happens in the family should be settled in the family. By extension, what happens in the community should be settled in the community.

Chinese Catholics would not have needed formal study to teach them this. It underlies the entire mentality of the Chinese and of guanxi. What, after all, is guanxi for but for the resolution of problems? Those who have it need never bring themselves before the authorities for problem resolution.

Like the Scots, in addition to familial and provincial relationships, the Chinese identify within their namesakes. These are called *clans*. They can be found in any sizable Chinese community in the world. In the United States, they have most commonly been called *benevolent associations*. The physical location of the benevolent association is called a *tong*, which simply means "hall," "classroom," or "gathering place." The word has unfortunately become affiliated with criminal gang activity as the result of undesirable elements within the Chinese community. Be that as it may, the clan's tong is actually a revered place.

These associations are open only to Chinese people who share a common surname. For instance, my surname, Lee, is the most common surname in the world. In addition to its commonality among Chinese, it happens to be common among the Koreans, the Vietnamese, and the English. But the Lee benevolent association is open only to Chinese people named Lee. I recall that my own father's initiation into the association was quite a cause for celebration.

What gives the tong reverence is that it offers the comfort of belonging, the beginning of any beautiful friendship. As a benevolent association, the stated purpose of the organization is to further the development of the clan. Therefore, from these associations, a simple guanxi network can be created. I believe Amway would approve of such tactics.

Economist Muhammad Yunus would probably approve of the associations for another reason. In 2006, he was awarded the Nobel Peace Prize for his life's work in extending tiny-sized loans to the most indigent people of Bangladesh, people who would not otherwise qualify for credit. This is known as *microfinance*. The clans have had a similar mechanism in place for centuries.

In the days when the Chinatowns of the world were not even safe to walk, obtaining credit was inconceivable. The clans filled this purpose admirably. As J. P. Morgan knew, the key to credit is the character of the borrower. Since the Chinese could not obtain credit conventionally, they could resort to the clan, the company of brothers who would indeed know their character. The start of many a small fortune among Chinese immigrants was derived from just such humble microfinancing.

But neither the clan nor the tong is the focus of this discussion. Both are useful because they serve a greater good. That good is the creation of guanxi. As we move further through the information age, I believe the relevance of the clan associations will decline as other means of creating guanxi become more efficient. But those of us who still have firsthand knowledge of their existence have an obligation to preserve their memory. They were an integral part of our history.

CASE STUDY: AIG

The story of the American International Group (AIG) of companies is stunning in its glory and tragedy. Notwithstanding that the company has fallen egregiously, the fact remains that for almost a century AIG ranked at the top of the corporate leagues by any measure. Business historians will note that at its apex, long before globalization became the buzzword, AIG had its hand in every country in the developed world as well as in most of the undeveloped world, including China. I consider the success of AIG in China to be an excellent case study of the value of establishing guanxi.

AIG had only two leaders for most of its storied history, both of whom were very skilled in cultivating guanxi networks. The first was its founder, Cornelius Vander Starr, a Californian who, like legions of others, was entranced by the business opportunities in China, not unlike today. Experienced only with insurance, he settled in Shanghai after World War I and founded the Starr insurance businesses.

Starr led his operations to great prosperity despite China's turbulence. Although Starr never learned to speak Chinese, his knowledge about China was extensive. Even more important, he had an uncanny ability to work with the local people. This was guanxi in action. Before Starr's arrival, foreigners in China kept to themselves in their enclave, suspicious and fearful of the Chinese. Naturally, this kept them from making the advances toward people which would engender guanxi relationships.

Starr did it differently. He went out to the people. Not speaking Chinese did not hinder him. He even managed to get elected to the Shanghai Municipal Council. Long before it was obvious to everyone else, he knew that strong ties to local people would prove critical to an enterprise's success. Not surprisingly, under his inspired leadership his insurance business in China flourished.

In World War II, as an ally of the United States, China, probably for the first time in its history, welcomed foreigners to repel the invading Japanese. Although China saw far too much bloodshed on its soil, the capitulation of the Japanese seemed to mark the rise of a strong American ally in the Far East.

It was not to be. Just four years after the end of World War II, Mao's guerrilla rebels turned the course of world history. His communist revolution in 1949 accomplished what the Japanese could not. It drove Starr out of China. Even in the wake of this, I suspect that Starr had intentions of returning and rebuilding his company. But he did not get the chance. He died in 1968.

The task of reentering China would fall to his successor, Maurice Greenberg. At the fledgling AIG created shortly before Starr's death, Greenberg was far ahead of his time in realizing the potential of the Chinese market even under communism. If C. V. Starr were the Babe Ruth of guanxi, Greenberg would be its Lou Gehrig. In 1975, he made his first visit to Beijing. Decades before other major American businesses would plan for the Chinese market, he had cemented his ties to the emerging group of Chinese leaders. Just five years later (an infinitesimal time period for the Chinese), AIG opened its new presence in Beijing, marking the return to the country that Starr had long coveted.

By the 1990s, Greenberg's government contacts had themselves prospered politically. In particular, former Shanghai mayor Zhu Rongji had risen to become the country's premier, China's second highest political office. Not surprisingly, AIG prospered further. Under Greenberg, despite intractable political tensions between the United States and China, AIG would work the guanxi route relentlessly. No political leader in either the United States or China was out of his reach. American presidents of either party could count on Greenberg's advice, knowing he knew the territory better than they did. Similarly, Chinese leaders could count on Greenberg for interpretations of political winds. I myself had business dealings with Greenberg early in my career and am still struck by the prescience of the man. Among so many other things, he created the world's first fund specifically to develop infrastructure in developing Asian nations.

The departure of Greenberg from AIG in 2005 under an unfounded cloud of suspicion was a great blow not just for AIG stockholders but for all American business and Sino-American relations in general. One cannot help wondering whether AIG would have gone under in 2008 if the iron hand of Greenberg had been on the company's wheel. Be that as it may, even in his late eighties, Greenberg remains vital. The guanxi he cultivated over many decades at AIG has been transferred to the Starr group of companies, which he continues to chair. One doesn't bet against a man of his ability, and if nothing else, his legacy to the rest of us is a shining example of guanxi done right.

CASE STUDY: HSBC

If AIG epitomized the successful implementation of guanxi from an American perspective, the Hong Kong and Shanghai Banking Corporation (HSBC) serves the same role for a British company. Founded inauspiciously in British-held Hong Kong in 1865, at the time of this writing, HSBC is the world's second largest financial institution. Just as AIG showed that it is possible to penetrate China's insular insurance market, HSBC has done the same for the banking market.

The Hong Kong of 1865 was nothing like the thriving, bustling global metropolis it is today. In point of fact, it was nothing. Nothing but a piece of land on the water. But in the wake of the First Opium War, Britain annexed it as a colony. As the war's name might suggest, it was over opium. Specifically, it was ostensibly over the right of the British to sell opium in China.

Once annexed, Hong Kong traders needed a bank to finance growing amounts of new trade, especially of opium. In stepped a Scotsman named Thomas Sutherland, who wanted to establish a bank on "sound Scottish banking principles." The creators of the Hong Kong and Shanghai Bank did a masterful job of blending the financial talents of the Hong Kong traders and the Scottish bankers.

The Scotsmen who ran the bank built up an Asian network brilliantly. A century before AIG would do so, HSBC was already establishing a pan-Asian presence. Such was the strength of its guanxi that it was soon issuing banknotes in both Hong Kong and Shanghai and eventually in Thailand as well. It continues to print bank notes in Hong Kong to this day. The idea that a private company could print its own currency frequently perplexes students who are more accustomed to the idea that a country's treasury is the issuing body of currency. But in fact, once business relationships are strong enough, there is no economic necessity for a treasury to do what can be contracted out to a trusted corporation.

From inception, despite Scottish management, the bank has operated as locally as any corporation has ever done. For instance, it has had a continuous presence in Shanghai since its founding, except for a brief interlude during the Japanese occupation during World War II.

Such loyalty is never forgotten among the Chinese. Therefore, in 2004, when the Shanghai-based Bank of Communications, China's fifth largest bank, decided to sell a stake to a foreign company, it was no surprise that HSBC was selected. The price of US$1.75 billion was eight times bigger than any previous foreign investment in a Chinese bank, and yet it was an amount that many of the world's financial institutions eager to expand into China's banking market would have paid. But it takes more than a top-dollar amount to win these bids. HSBC had a trump card. It had guanxi.

SUMMARY

The critical lesson of this chapter is that the creation of a relationship system like a guanxi network can be very rewarding in dealing with the Chinese. However, even when not dealing with the Chinese, the idea that a network of reliable business contacts be made is still a valuable business strategy.

But let's be clear. This lesson must be applied very judiciously. I'm aware that it is often considered crass in the West to expect repayment for a favor. But that does not mean that strong bonds of familiarity cannot be created. And that's the key.

First, do the favors. In fact, seek out opportunities to do them. Not for any mercenary or Machiavellian purpose, but also not just out of the goodness of your heart. Before long, something approximating a guanxi bond will have been created. Top salespeople in any field know this intuitively. They ferret out opportunities to perform a good turn, thereby establishing a likelihood that the recipient will at least listen to a sales pitch at an appropriate time in the future. Bingo! Guanxi strikes. This is the third principle of the Chinese Way to Wealth and Prosperity.

CHAPTER FOUR

KEEP DEBT TO AN ABSOLUTE MINIMUM

In the winter of 2011, a television commercial from an organization called Citizens Against Government Waste caused a bit of a stir. In it, a professor speaking in Chinese lectures his students about the inevitable fall of empires. He compared great civilizations from the ancient Greeks to the modern United States. All were magnificent in their day. But in the end, all great civilizations crumble, he said. The professor concluded by saying that excessive debt was the primary reason for the fall of all these empires. Referring to the tremendous amount of American debt held by China, he punctuated his conclusion by stating that now the United States works for China.

Later that year, on August 5, 2011, to be precise, a very grim turning point in U.S. history was reached because on that day the United States lost its beloved AAA credit rating, the highest available. The downgrade by the rating agency Standard & Poor's was the first since the United States was granted a rating all the way back in 1917. It was not entirely unexpected though. The overhang from trillions upon trillions of dollars of debt had been much commented upon for months. But it was a severe blow nevertheless.

While the full ramifications of the downgrade will be felt for years, the immediate lesson is already obvious. Even as the United States has been drowning in debt, China has been building itself into a superpower without it. It's a curious time in history. The single most powerful nation in the world now finds itself in deep hock to a developing one.

There is cause for concern, though not panic. The United States still has the largest and most diverse economy in the world even if China is gaining fast. But it is about time to heed the lesson. The United States is able to retain its position despite its tremendous debt, not because of it. We as individuals cannot and must not expect a similar luxury in handling our personal finances. I believe the example of the United States government should serve as fair warning to anyone who seeks personal prosperity.

THE DISCONTENT OF DEBT, PART 1

Didn't our parents warn us about the dangers of borrowing? Whether or not we attend church, the proverb about the borrower being the slave of the lender stands generally true. Any way we cut it, the United States has managed its fiscal house terribly. The downgrade itself is less important than the reason given for it. Given the tremendous amount of debt issued by the United States, Standard & Poor's wanted to see an appropriate plan for the management of it and for the consequent payment of over $400 billion per year just in interest costs. Standard & Poor's was unable to determine one.

It is beyond the scope of this book to advise the administration on its next steps. I expect that a full army of academics and bureaucrats will be working overtime to resolve the national debt problem. It is far more important to emphasize the lesson that China has in store for us. If the United States comes across as a negative example of fiscal management, China comes across as a shining positive one.

China did not precipitate our country's debt crisis. In fact, a good case could be made that the U.S. Treasury should thank China for being so generous with its checkbook. How generous? According to official figures at the time of this writing, the People's Republic of China holds over $1 trillion in U.S. Treasury bonds. But unofficial figures, which include Chinese ownership of U.S. corporate debt as well, swell the total to over $2 trillion. To say the least, that's a lot of money.

THE DISCONTENT OF DEBT, PART 2

As if the national debt crisis weren't bad enough, the United States also faces a debt crisis at the consumer level. News reports sometimes conflate the two, but it is important to note that we in the United States are actually fighting debt wars on two separate fronts. The national debt, which is the debt of the U.S. Treasury, is analogous to money owed by your landlord. Ostensibly, the landlord's debt, such as the mortgage loan used to buy the house, is none of the tenant's business. However, it does become the tenant's business if, as the result of overborrowing, the landlord's costs of borrowing rise. In a typical real estate transaction, these higher costs get passed on to the tenants in the form of future rental increases. By similar logic, this is why our national debt crisis affects all of us. That debt must be paid somehow. And it may well happen that we, the "tenants" of the United States, must eventually pay "rental" increases in the form of taxes.

Unfortunately, there isn't much we can do about the national debt other than vote for responsible politicians. But there is indeed much that we can and must do about debt at the personal level. If anything, the reported numbers for personal debt are even more frightening than for the national debt. In 2010, total consumer debt in the United States amounted to a staggering $2.5 trillion! This works out to approximately $7,800 in debt for every man, woman, and child who lives in the United States. Perhaps even more worrisome, a full third of this $2.5 trillion is in the form of credit card balances, quite possibly the worst kind of credit available.

Not bad enough? Actually, the data get worse. Unfortunately, the $2.5 trillion does not include mortgage loans. These amounted to a further $14 trillion. A case can and will be made for the necessity of mortgage debt, but the fact remains that even at the personal level, the United States is in well over its head. The situation is unsustainable.

THE ENCUMBERED AMERICAN

How did this happen to our country? Surely this is not part of the American dream. No people immigrating to our country could possibly have had this in mind for their futures. For generations of immigrants, the dream was to come to America and build a good life. This dream was all the more beautiful because of its sheer attainability. But building a good life is significantly harder if one is buried under a mountain of debt. Could it be that we have forgotten how to build a good life?

To some extent, I believe the answer is yes. Politicians and economists might lay the blame on monetary policy or on regulatory lapses, but I take a different view. In the end, I believe there was a tremendous crisis of personal responsibility. Whatever missteps were made at the federal level, the fact remains that people are individually responsible for their finances. In permitting our personal finances to veer so far off the cliff, we as a nation became derelict in our responsibility to ourselves.

I believe this dereliction of responsibility is the true tragedy. Prosperity is built upon the investment of capital, including the all-important human capital. But somewhere along the way, our mindset changed to one that suggested that it was acceptable to borrow so far beyond our means. In so doing, while losing much of our financial capital, we also lost a great chunk of our human capital, our very humanity.

The nationwide financial crisis, dire as it clearly was, was merely the result of this far greater malaise. At this point, we do not need government solutions. Far more important is for us to regain this facet of our human capital, this sense of personal responsibility for our finances.

Let's return to the commercial ad mentioned at the beginning of this chapter. Controversial though it may have been, its underlying logic is not wrong. If you owe money to someone, you are in fact working to pay that someone back. Fortunately, we don't have indentured servitude anymore, but especially for people like the Chinese who have some history of bonded service, the idea of indebtedness is particularly repellant. This has clearly not been the case in the United States. I believe it would very much behoove us individually and collectively to adopt the Chinese attitude toward debt.

OWNING UP

So right at the outset, it is critically important to own up to our own culpability. This is no time for outward blame. No one likes banks, but unless the banks literally forced us to take their money, they don't hold primary responsibility for the predicament we're in.

I'm fully aware how aggressive their marketing can be. I'm also very aware that their interest rate disclosures could be clearer. But at the end of the day, the fact remains that we chose to accept the debt. Therefore, we must hold ourselves responsible. This is as important in personal finance as it is in a 12-step recovery program for alcoholics. It's the critical first step to recovery from anything.

Railing against the banks may be cathartic. It may release steam. It may even be fun. But one thing it won't be is helpful. Don't waste any time like this. It may even prove counterproductive if we find ourselves hating them enough to avoid paying them back. That only makes our bad situation worse.

AN INVESTMENT IN YOURSELF

Our course of action should be very clear. We should, at all costs, release ourselves from the encumbrance of our debt. I doubt any of us don't know this, but we still haven't acted. I believe part of the reason we haven't acted is that the thought of repaying debt sounds inadequately motivating. I suppose many of us would far prefer to keep our debt in place while we spend or invest our money elsewhere. If that is the case, I recommend that the problem be looked at another way. Consider money spent paying down debt as an investment in yourself and a repurchase of your human capital. You are buying back your freedom.

This point bears repeating. Don't think of repaying debt as parting with your precious money to an impersonal financial institution. That won't spur anyone to act. Think of it instead as buying something of great value. What you will have bought are the keys to your financial freedom.

Let's face facts. Heeding the other lessons in this book will bring wealth sooner or later, but not if the gains are consumed by increasing amounts of debt.

There is a common metric used in the field of finance. It's called *return on investment*. Its calculation is simple enough. You only need to divide the gain you achieved (the numerator) by the amount of capital invested (the denominator). We can use this formulation to approximate a return on investment of our human capital. We may remember from our grade school arithmetic that it is meaningless to divide any number by zero. I think the lesson is quite appropriate. It would be similarly meaningless to strive for prosperity if we fritter away our human capital so that a return on investment cannot be calculated. We need to recover it.

RETURNS WITHOUT RISK

This section's heading doesn't seem to make sense, does it? Most people are familiar with the fundamental trade-off between risk and return. In order to obtain a high rate of return, it stands to reason that a high degree of risk must be accepted. This is generally true. But the principle of debt repayment constitutes an exception of sorts to this general principle.

Let's look at the numbers. Consider someone with $10,000 in credit card debt. If the person has a spare dollar, let's ask what he'd consider a great return without risk. I would guess that we'd hear an answer like 5 percent or so. Well, if the person feels 5 percent is a great return, shouldn't he jump at the chance to earn 19.99 percent without risk? Actually, that can be accomplished very easily.

Since typical credit card balances accrue interest at the rate of 19.99 percent per year, the person would have to earn at least that much with the spare dollar just to stay in place. That's a very tall order. But its equivalent can be achieved simply by using the spare dollar to reduce some of the debt. In so doing, the interest expense on that dollar which will not have to be paid constitutes a return on investment on the dollar, and a very high one at that.

Now let's assume that the person in question considers himself an investment genius and wishes to "outearn" the credit card's 19.99 percent interest rate. The logic is fair enough on the surface. But returning to the risk-return trade-off, the person would very quickly find himself encroaching on some very high-risk territory if he attempted this. Risk, of course, means that high returns might not necessarily materialize. Returns may even be negative. If that happens, the person will lose money even as the 19.99 percent interest costs accumulate. So much for the investment genius.

Or alternatively, and far more easily, the person can earn 19.99 percent without risk simply by paying down the credit card balance. For the person with credit card debt, there is literally no better investment in personal finance than this.

Actually, this investment in itself gets better than this. Even if the investment genius succeeded in defying the odds and the risks and earned 19.99 percent, it would be subject to tax. That means he'd have to aim even higher than 19.99 percent just to have the 19.99 percent after the IRS gets its share. Assuming that our hypothetical genius was in the 25 percent tax bracket, he'd actually need to earn a 26.67 percent return on his money in order to have 19.99 percent left over to pay the card's interest rate. With numbers like this, we enter the land of Alice in Wonderland. The better choice is pretty clear. There simply is no better investment than the repurchase of your human capital via the repayment of debt.

BAD DEBT VERSUS REGRETTABLY NECESSARY DEBT

The sheer scope of the numbers at the national and personal levels is admittedly overwhelming. But that certainly cannot be allowed to dissuade people from the task at hand, which is to reduce their personal debt obligations. It may help, however, to fine-tune the numbers a bit. Not all debt is the same.

Many financial advisors distinguish between good debt and bad debt. For optimum impact, though, I would suggest a slight change in terminology. It's a semantic point but an important one. To the Chinese mind, it simply goes against the grain to call any borrowing, however well targeted, good.

There is only bad debt and what I call regrettably necessary debt (RND).

The emphasis can be useful. Debt can be appropriate. Debt can be necessary. Debt is always regrettable. But debt can never be truly good. Putting it in such stark terms may bring us some distance toward recovery.

RND refers to borrowing for specific purposes that have the potential to create wealth. Determining exactly how much debt is necessary in the field of corporate finance can be tricky, but it is much clearer in personal finance. For instance, few people would disagree that taking out a mortgage loan to purchase a home represents necessary debt. There just aren't that many of us who can buy a home with cash. But more to the point, a properly maintained home can legitimately be expected to appreciate in value over time. Thus, mortgage loans are very much RND.

In many cases, a student loan can also be considered RND, because as we saw in Chapter 1, proper education can raise your income potential and hence your future wealth. Both mortgage loans and student loans represent the kind of necessary borrowing that most people would support.

Bad debt, on the other hand, is debt incurred for most every other purpose. Unfortunately, this kind of debt seems to run rampant in our society. What makes it bad is that no wealth can reasonably be expected to be created from it. A loan to finance a new car, for instance, is bad debt. Cars, even the best of them, decline in value over time. Similarly, loans for the purchase of clothes, electronics, vacations, etc., are examples of bad debt. That's not to say that those expenditures are entirely useless. But such expenditures should more properly be paid out of one's current income, not with borrowed money.

Some people will try to use the argument that such spending may enhance your ability to earn more. That argument leads you down a very slippery slope in which any indulgence can be rationalized away as an "investment" in yourself. Don't fall for that. As a general rule, debt incurred from buying anything at a mall should be considered bad debt. Here's another general rule: the higher the rate of interest you have to pay, the worse the debt is.

Consider interest from the lender's perspective. Why would a lender charge different rates for different loans? The lender is not in the business of giving money away, and so it must assess different rates depending on the risk of the loan. Safer loans, like mortgage loans in which the borrower truly has much to lose by defaulting, can be assessed a lower interest rate because of the greater security involved. What we've just called bad debt, on the other hand, is not secured by anything. The lenders rely on the borrower's good faith to repay. Therefore, to compensate for taking the higher risk entailed in extending those loans, lenders must charge a higher interest rate. This means a double whammy for bad debt borrowers. First, they've borrowed for something that does not increase their wealth, and second, the cost of that borrowing is significantly higher than for RND.

THE TERROR OF BAD DEBT

There's no way around it. We need to declare war on bad debt. And to accomplish it, there is one and only one way. Don't let anyone try to convince you otherwise. You could buy a hundred books and hire a dozen financial advisors, and the conclusion will be the same in the end. It's simply this: every month, you must pay off more than is minimally due. That's it. Rocket science is not required. If you can get the lender to lower your rate of interest, that's great. If you can cajole the lender to forgive part of the loan, that's even better. But you will still have to deal with the loan that remains.

As mentioned earlier in this chapter, the critical first step is to see debt repayment as an investment in ourselves. The equally critical second step is to focus on how much we're hurting ourselves by making only what lenders require as minimum payments. The Credit Card Act signed by President Obama in May of 2009 now requires such information to be put into credit card bills.

Let's consider the example of someone owing $10,000 in credit card debt at an interest rate of 19.99 percent. Typically, the minimum payment is 3 percent of the balance owed. If you merely made the minimum monthly payment of 3 percent, you would not retire this debt for, believe it or not, 90 years!

A lengthy mathematical illustration is not necessary. You can intuit why it takes so long. Even as you pay down the minimum 3 percent per month, interest continues to accrue on the balance at the rate of approximately 1.67 percent per month (which is roughly 19.99 percent per year divided by 12). It's almost precisely like taking one step forward (3 percent paid down) followed by half a step back (1.67 percent more interest).

This is clearly not the way to wealth. Minimum required payments are the scourge of prosperity. They leave a misleading impression that one is making progress toward reducing debt. People do over the course of a very long time, but it comes at a very steep cost.

Most people will not have the ability to repay all their debts at once, or presumably they would have done so. But a great deal could be accomplished just by making slightly more than the minimum required payments.

Consider how the numbers change if you could find an additional $2 a day that could be dedicated to repaying debt. That would be $60 per month on top of the minimum required 3 percent payment. If you did as little as that, you would find that you'd extinguish the debt in just over 7 years. That's right—an additional $60 per month reduces the life of your credit card debt from over 90 years to 7 years. Doesn't it seem worthwhile? I doubt most people would have great trouble finding $2 a day.

Let's take it up a notch. Now let's assume you can find $5 a day, or $150 per month, in addition to the 3 percent required minimum payment. Admittedly, $150 might be more difficult to find. But notice how much more the numbers change. Now the debt gets retired in only 4 years. Seeing these numbers in the light of day just might provide the motivating spark.

For the even more ambitious, let's assume that $10 a day can be found, or $300 more per month. This would definitely sting. You'd probably have to eat out a few times less per month, but the rewards are great. After running the numbers, you would find that the debt is retired even more quickly in only 27 months, less than 3 years.

Whether or not you can find the additional $10 per day, the point is clear and obvious. Making only required minimum payments is the way to lingering indebtedness. On the other hand, consistently stretching yourself to make just a bit larger payment puts you on the path to eventual debt elimination.

PREPAYING YOUR MORTGAGE?

There should be no question that the reduction of unsecured consumer credit must be the first order of business. However, it becomes a little more iffy when we turn our attention to our mortgage loan. Just as with credit card debt, the total amount of interest that accrues over the years on a mortgage loan is gargantuan. But there are important additional considerations.

The first point to emphasize is that mortgage reduction should not be considered until all your nonmortgage debt has been extinguished. In all likelihood, your mortgage loan will have the lowest interest rate of all your outstanding debts. It is just common sense to leave a lower interest debt in place until all higher interest debt is fully repaid.

But what happens when your mortgage loan is your only debt remaining? Then it becomes a judgment call. You can even consider it a pleasant problem in that the situation could only have arisen from having successfully repaid all your other debt.

Let's return to the example of the investment genius mentioned earlier. Suppose this person has a 5 percent mortgage loan with no other debt. Should this person use available savings to prepay the mortgage?

On the surface, it seems very possible to outearn the interest rate on the mortgage loan. In fact, the task is even easier. The 5 percent stated rate is not the true rate since interest paid on a mortgage loan is deductible from your taxes. Assuming the person is in the 25 percent tax bracket, the after-tax cost of debt falls from 5 percent to merely 3.75 percent.

This seems like a low enough hurdle. But we must take a good hard look at ourselves before concluding that we can absolutely beat this hurdle rate. Will we be able to suffer through the inevitable downturns in the investment markets? A rate of 3.75 percent isn't so easy to beat when the stock markets themselves are imploding, as they are doing with increasing frequency. At times like that, will you have the perseverance to stay the course and await the market to swing back up? Or will you kick yourself for not having earned the 3.75 percent by simply repaying mortgage debt?

There is another consideration, a psychological one. A mortgage loan may be RND, but your home is not just another impersonal financial instrument. There is a very critical difference between our house and every other investment. We love our homes. We care for them and treat them as cherished possessions. In contrast, although financial advisors warn people against falling in love with particular investments, it's just a figure of speech. Not many people actually fall in love with a company's stock as they would their house. Now consider, if you love something this much, would you not desire to unencumber it from the bonds of debt? Wouldn't it give you great pleasure to unencumber yourself from the debt that binds such a treasured possession? In the past, people held parties upon making the final payment on their mortgages for just this reason. Only you can answer the question, but many do choose to do so for just this psychological reason. And the savings in interest costs would be tremendous.

SUMMARY

The main point of this chapter was to illustrate the role that debt plays in inhibiting wealth creation. It is never too late to learn this lesson. The task of reducing our debts will be a difficult one, but it must be started. We can only hope that our elected officials will take the necessary steps regarding the national debt. But there is no excuse for us not to attack our personal debt. This is the fourth principle of the Chinese Way to Wealth and Prosperity.

Chapter Five

Play
Financial
Defense

Although I believe every lesson in this book is an important one on the path to prosperity, the specific lesson contained in this chapter stands alone in its simplicity. There is little excuse for not benefiting from playing financial defense. Regrettably, far too frequently in the United States, this lesson seems to have been ignored completely.

If nothing else, the recent Great Recession revealed a terrible fault line in the American economy. Just as geographic fault lines cause untold damage to an affected area when an earthquake hits, a financial fault line causes tremendous damage to our financial well-being when the equivalent of an earthquake hits the economy. In our recent downturn, that was precisely what happened.

The total costs of the devastation are still not known, but the anecdotes are heartbreaking. The tales of homes foreclosed upon and retirement accounts decimated flowed unceasingly from the newspapers and financial press. No one can fail to be moved by the desperation of honest workers reduced to poverty by the economic crisis.

In truth, it should not have taken the Great Recession to get us to learn this lesson. Surely, we had all been taught since childhood about the importance of saving, but apparently many of us chose to ignore it. When the financial crisis hit the world, there was no ignoring it any longer. The sad truth was revealed. We simply did not save enough during the good times because we expected them to roll forever.

But I believe it is never too late to learn any lesson. I even believe that we can eventually regain our losses if we learn our lesson now. However, all would be truly lost, including our futures, if after the devastation that has been caused, we still do not learn. It is my hope that this chapter will do its part in helping Americans back onto the road to recovery and then onward to prosperity.

THE ROOT OF ALL WEALTH

The undeniable truth is that from time immemorial, there has been one sure way to ensure personal prosperity. This one-way ticket to prosperity has been the consistent saving of a portion of one's earnings. It's been called the American way, but lately I feel that non-Americans have learned this lesson better than we have in this country.

To judge from our nation's spending and investing habits, far too many people seem to believe that the path to prosperity involves a big winner in the stock market or a winning lottery ticket. It would be wonderful if that were true, but the harsh truth is that either scenario is beyond unlikely. Delusional would be more accurate.

I do not in any way denigrate stock market investing (although I certainly do denigrate lotteries). But it must be kept in mind that stock investing is far from a sure bet. Missing from the business press, which loves to report on stock market home runs, are millions of untold stories about losses suffered by ordinary people and even by professionals in the stock market. Such stories exist even when times are good. But when times are bad, they proliferate tragically.

No one can deny the allure of stock trading. Who doesn't dream of buying the stock that doubles or quadruples quickly? Who doesn't lust for the appeal of repeated gains day after day? That's certainly the reason why day trading was so popular for a while. And for a while, it can indeed look great, like when the stock market is roaring ahead. At such times, people feel that they are true gifts to the financial marketplace. Everything they touch seemingly turns to gold. At least on paper, fortunes are made, but unfortunately are then spent.

Good times never last forever. Whether we like it or not, sooner or later, the market gyrates downward. At that point, the hopes, dreams, and perceived assurances of wealth are dashed. Much of the gains could possibly have been recouped in the long term, but understandably, many people will have been too badly burned to stick around.

It doesn't have to be this way. If we'd return to basics, we'd stand a far better chance to become wealthy. It's the tried-and-true method of steady and consistent saving. It requires great discipline though, which may be why it's never been popular. However, if generations of new immigrants know to apply it, there's no reason why Americans can't also.

CHEAP OR WISE?

In my professional career, I have had the privilege of traveling to many countries. Whenever possible, I make an attempt to visit a city's Chinatown. There are far more of these than most people realize. One memorable summer, I even had the pleasure of visiting the Chinatown in Budapest, Hungary, which apparently thrived even behind the iron curtain.

Given the peripatetic nature of the Chinese over the centuries, it may not be surprising that Chinese communities have sprung up all over the globe. And given the appeal of big cities for immigrants from any country, it wouldn't be surprising that metropolises spawn some of the largest Chinatowns. But these Chinatowns also spring up in some truly unexpected places. Who would have guessed that there are even Chinatowns in Israel, Dubai, and Serbia?

None of the little Chinatowns can match the size of San Francisco's, Toronto's, or New York's, which are almost small cities in themselves, but they do share the big Chinatowns' basic characteristics. First, Chinatowns have a plethora of dragon, panda, and pagoda imagery. Some people may find this tacky, but this type of decorative splendor usually helps bring in the outsiders. Second, Chinatowns function simultaneously as tourist attraction and community center for the local Chinese population. Third, the restaurant trade, which provides much local employment, is a substantial portion of the real estate. And finally, and most to the point, Chinatowns almost always maintain an aura of frugality. Although there is always a grand restaurant somewhere in the mix, many of the others are cut-rate, buy-and-run eateries. The same goes for most of the retail establishments.

We might as well just call them cheap. I do not feel that word is a term of denigration. I think no offense should be taken. In fact, I personally might even trumpet the designation. That's because for the purpose of achieving prosperity, cheapness is an incredibly valuable trait. I see no point in drawing a sharp distinction between *cheap* and that word's more respectable sounding cousins, *thrifty* and *frugal*. They all essentially mean the same thing: not overspending. Not overspending, not even on what may be considered essential to others, is the name of the game. And the Chinese play this game very, very well.

THE IRREFUTABLE TRUTH

The numbers don't lie. The U.S. savings rate has declined steadily over the past three decades. It even went negative in 2006 for the first time since the Great Depression, before settling at a middling 5 percent of income. This is truly depressing. In contrast, the household savings rate in China, already high at 16 percent of disposable income in 1990, has rocketed to over 30 percent in recent years.

This 30 percent figure pertained to people in China, but the situation is not much different among Chinese immigrants to the United States. According to economists Jing Xiao of the University of Rhode Island and Jessie Fan of the University of Utah, immigrants from China have an average savings rate that is about 11 percent higher than that of native-born Americans after holding constant age, education, occupation, and duration of stay in the United States.

In addition, the professors found that for Chinese immigrants, the longer the duration of their stay in the United States, the higher their savings rate. I would attribute this to the greater amount of money that is earned as immigrants stay longer in this country. The fact is inescapable; something is definitely afoot in the Chinese culture regarding savings.

This dynamic has not gone unnoticed by the banks. For instance, in New York City's original Chinatown, the 15 to

20 percent savings rate of the residents there has attracted more than 40 banking establishments, accumulating more than $7 billion in deposits in an area not much bigger than a dozen city blocks! This speaks well for the banks, but it speaks even better for the depositors. They have truly financially empowered themselves.

THE WHY OF CHINESE FRUGALITY, PART 1

Growing up, I often wondered why my parents were so keenly attuned to saving. I couldn't see why they were so unwilling to spend, especially on me. This was a very selfish motive to be sure, but it was an inescapable part of my upbringing. After all, in my naïveté, I assumed money was earned to be spent.

In time, I would learn to appreciate how my mother could stretch a dollar past its breaking point, but I never truly understood it. After I entered the workforce, I could also not understand how I could never approach my parents' savings rate even though they never earned even half of my first year's income. It all comes down to mindset.

Not surprisingly, Confucian values were the major factor. The critical teaching of relevance was a general injunction from Confucius to be prudent, "as if you were standing at the edge of a cliff or walking on a thin layer of ice." Notice that this was not necessarily a financial prescription. It was an admonishment to be careful in all areas of life. However, I believe the wisdom contained in this one saying has influenced Chinese people for generations, even those who may never have heard the original quotation.

Beneath the surface of the saying was a clear implication. In any area of life, one who walks on a thin layer of ice must prepare for a breakage of that ice and therefore must take appropriate precaution. In the area of household finances, this precaution supplies the motive for the hefty savings rate. Immigrant Chinese like my own parents knew to heed the sage's advice.

THE WHY OF CHINESE FRUGALITY, PART 2

Recent Chinese history provides another explanation. Although China has indeed experienced marvelous economic growth since embarking upon the capitalist path 30 years ago, there has been upheaval in some formerly sacred areas. The principle of the "iron rice bowl," a euphemistic way of saying that food would always be available, no longer applies in modern China. It's debatable if it ever did, but at least in theory, the communist system was supposed to provide at least basic sustenance for its citizens. But the advent of capitalism in China starting in the late 1970s meant that many enterprises that were formerly state owned would henceforth be on their own.

Even if the iron rice bowl had been slightly cracked at times, this new phenomenon had dramatic consequences for the workers who had been reasonably confident where their next meal would come from. It didn't take long for the workers to see the writing on the wall. This economic transformation kicked the Chinese savings engine into even higher gear.

Helping the cause was the government's new attitude toward Confucianism. Formerly seen as archaic and reactionary under communism, Confucianism had become accepted once again in China for the stability it lends to society. In fact, the Chinese government has funded hundreds of Confucius Institutes around the world to disseminate the principles of Chinese language and culture. In so doing, the government has helped to revive the values that animate traditional Confucianism, including a prudent frugality.

Economic reform has also changed the mode of home ownership. In the old system, housing in China (such as it was) was provided and rationed by the government. But this too has changed. Private and better housing options are now available. A great influx of people desiring new housing very quickly creates a tremendous accumulation of savings.

The combination of all these factors has given American politicians fuel for political rhetoric. Some have been known to berate the Chinese for saving too much and spending too little. This is laughable. I, for one, would not take their advice to heart. The savings dynamic in China has been unleashed, and the Chinese have already seen the fruits of their frugality. It remains for us to learn from their example.

THE CURE: EINSTEIN'S WONDERMENT

Fortunately, the lesson is very easy to learn. It only involves one principle. It is the principle of compound interest. No less an eminence than Albert Einstein has proclaimed that the most powerful force in the universe is compound interest. Einstein is also credited with having said that compound interest is the greatest mathematical discovery of all time. This, from the creator of the theory of relativity, cannot be ignored.

And, in fact, there's no underestimating the importance of compound interest. The saving of money is the sown seed, but compound interest is the water and sunshine that makes that seed grow into a full crop.

Let's start with some basic math. Suppose you have managed to save $1.00 (congratulations). If you invest it at a flat 10 percent, you would get the saved dollar back, plus $0.10 (10 cents) in interest, for a total of $1.10. Not terrible, but not exciting either. But suppose you left the money invested for a second year. If the interest rate remains at 10 percent, how much interest would you gain in the second year? The intuitive answer of another 10 cents would not be correct. That's because in the second year, the amount on which the 10 percent would be applied is no longer $1.00 but $1.10. Thus, at the end of the second year, you would gain $0.11, not just another $0.10, giving you a new total of $1.21. This $0.01 difference reflects the compounding of interest.

In this example, the difference is admittedly minimal. But let's continue the experiment for a third year. In that third year, you would earn another 10 percent on top of the 2-year total of $1.21. That would be an addition of $0.12, rather than $0.10. Perhaps you can start to see where this leads.

Now let's put a few zeros behind the numbers and extend the time frame for some real perspective and compare again.

Imagine that you have the more reasonable sum of $1,000 saved and could invest it at 10 percent per year for 10 years. What you would earn is not just $100 per year for 10 years, or $1,000. Similar to the previous example, the interest gained is only $100 for the first year. After the first year, the compounding factor kicks in, and kicks in hard. See Table 5-1 for the precise growth of the numbers. Earning 10 percent on a $1,000 investment actually yields $2,593.74 after 10 years. The additional $593.74 is due to the miracle of compound interest.

If the effect of compound interest starts looking impressive, you ain't seen nothing yet. Let's consider a more realistic example. An employee graduates from college at 22 and retires at 66. Suppose the worker saves $1,000, at a 10 percent interest rate, in the first working year and not a cent after that. What would that $1,000 be worth at retirement for the worker?

TABLE 5-1

AGE	THE YEAR'S INVESTMENT, $	BEGINNING-OF-YEAR VALUE, $	INTEREST AT 10%, $	END-OF YEAR-VALUE, $
22	1,000.00	1,000.00	100.00	1,100.00
23		1,100.00	110.00	1,210.00
24		1,210.00	121.00	1,331.00
25		1,331.00	133.10	1,464.10
26		1,464.10	146.41	1,610.51
27		1,610.51	161.05	1,771.56
28		1,771.56	177.16	1,948.72
29		1,948.72	194.87	2,143.59
30		2,143.59	214.36	2,357.95
31		2,357.95	235.79	2,593.74

In all my years of teaching, when I've posed this question on the first day of my finance classes, I have never had even one student come within half of the correct answer. In actuality, that original $1,000 would grow to $72,890! (See Table 5-2.) Perhaps we can start to appreciate what Einstein meant.

TABLE 5-2

AGE	THE YEAR'S INVESTMENT, $	BEGINNING-OF-YEAR VALUE, $	INTEREST AT 10%, $	END-OF YEAR-VALUE, $
22	1,000.00	1,000.00	100.00	1,100.00
23		1,100.00	110.00	1,210.00
24		1,210.00	121.00	1,331.00
25		1,331.00	133.10	1,464.10
26		1,464.10	146.41	1,610.51
27		1,610.51	161.05	1,771.56
28		1,771.56	177.16	1,948.72
29		1,948.72	194.87	2,143.59
30		2,143.59	214.36	2,357.95
31		2,357.95	235.79	2,593.74
32		2,593.74	259.37	2,853.12
33		2,853.12	285.31	3,138.43
34		3,138.43	313.84	3,452.27
35		3,452.27	345.23	3,797.50
36		3,797.50	379.75	4,177.25
37		4,177.25	417.72	4,594.97
38		4,594.97	459.50	5,054.47
39		5,054.47	505.45	5,559.92

(continued)

AGE	THE YEAR'S INVESTMENT, $	BEGINNING-OF- YEAR VALUE, $	INTEREST AT 10%, $	END-OF YEAR-VALUE, $
40		5,559.92	555.99	6,115.91
41		6,115.91	611.59	6,727.50
42		6,727.50	672.75	7,400.25
43		7,400.25	740.02	8,140.27
44		8,140.27	814.03	8,954.30
45		8,954.30	895.43	9,849.73
46		9,849.73	984.97	10,834.71
47		10,834.71	1,083.47	$11,918.18
48		11,918.18	1,191.82	$13,109.99
49		13,109.99	1,311.00	$14,420.99
50		14,420.99	1,442.10	15,863.09
51		15,863.09	1,586.31	17,449.40
52		17,449.40	1,744.94	19,194.34
53		19,194.34	1,919.43	21,113.78
54		21,113.78	2,111.38	23,225.15
55		23,225.15	2,322.52	25,547.67
56		25,547.67	2,554.77	28,102.44
57		28,102.44	2,810.24	30,912.68
58		30,912.68	3,091.27	34,003.95
59		34,003.95	3,400.39	37,404.34
60		37,404.34	3,740.43	41,144.78
61		41,144.78	4,114.48	45,259.26
62		45,259.26	4,525.93	49,785.18
63		49,785.18	4,978.52	54,763.70
64		54,763.70	5,476.37	60,240.07
65		60,240.07	6,024.01	66,264.08
66		66,264.08	6,626.41	72,890.48

Just about every finance textbook uses this next example. It's the story about how much Peter Minuit paid the Native Americans for the island of Manhattan in 1626. As legend has it, the amount was $24. It is fascinating to consider what the Native Americans could have reaped by employing the concept of compound interest. Here it is: if the Native Americans had been able to invest the $24 at 10 percent per year for the ensuing 385 years, they would currently have $207,202,517,436,662,000! This number is pronounced two hundred and seven quadrillion dollars and change. (The change alone amounts to over $202 trillion.) For comparison, consider that the entire gross domestic product of the United States in 2010 was (merely) $14.7 trillion.

EINSTEIN'S WONDERMENT APPLIED

To see how applicable this principle can be for our personal finances, consider the hypothetical example of a new college graduate who has the wherewithal to set aside $1,000 each of her first 10 working years. For a recent graduate who has housing and student loan payments to bear, this amount may stretch the budget but should not be undoable. If the graduate could achieve a 10 percent rate of return in each of these years, she would have a nice total of $17, 531 at the end of 10 years, as Table 5-3 shows.

This is already not bad. But the best part comes if the amount is left untouched and invested at 10 percent until the graduate retires. Let us assume again that the graduate retires

TABLE 5-3

AGE	THE YEAR'S INVESTMENT, $	BEGINNING-OF-YEAR VALUE, $	INTEREST AT 10%, $	END-OF YEAR-VALUE, $
22	1,000.00	1,000.00	100.00	1,100.00
23	1,000.00	2,100.00	210.00	2,310.00
24	1,000.00	3,310.00	331.00	3,641.00
25	1,000.00	4,641.00	464.10	5,105.10
26	1,000.00	6,105.10	610.51	6,715.61
27	1,000.00	7,715.61	771.56	8,487.17
28	1,000.00	9,487.17	948.72	10,435.89
29	1,000.00	11,435.89	1,143.59	12,579.48
30	1,000.00	13,579.48	1,357.95	14,937.42
31	1,000.00	15,937.42	1,593.74	17,53t.l7

at age 66, which gives the money 44 years to compound. At that time, the sum grows to a whopping $492,668! Remember that this person only invested a total of $10,000, $1,000 per year for 10 years. All the rest of the money is attributable to compound interest. As we can see, time truly is money.

Table 5-4 illustrates the growth of the money over the course of the years. Note how rapidly the money grows even after the graduate ceases to invest any more money. At age 66, for instance, the interest earned is nearly $45,000. Many new graduates will balk at parting with $1,000 every year at that point in their lives. This may be understandable but is unwise. These new workers will assume that they can make up for the lost time in later years. This is possible, but they face a greater and greater task the longer they wait to

TABLE 5-4

AGE	THE YEAR'S INVESTMENT, $	BEGINNING-OF-YEAR VALUE, $	INTEREST AT 10%, $	END-OF YEAR-VALUE, $
22	1,000.00	1,000.00	100.00	1,100.00
23	1,000.00	2,100.00	210.00	2,310.00
24	1,000.00	3,310.00	331.00	3,641.00
25	1,000.00	4,641.00	464.10	5,105.10)
26	1,000.00	6,105.10	610.51	6,715.61
27	1,000.00	7,715.61	771.56	8,487.17
28	1,000.00	9,487.17	948.72	10,435.89
29	1,000.00	11,435.89	1,143.59	12,579.48
30	1,000.00	13,579.48	1,357.95	14,937.42
31	1,000.00	15,937.42	1,593.74	17,531.17
32		17,531.17	1,753.12	19,284.28
33		19,284.28	1,928.43	21,212.71
34		21,212.71	2,121.27	23,333.98
35		23,333.98	2,333.40	25,667.38
36		25,667.38	2,566.74	28,234.12
37		28,234.12	2,823.41	31,057.53
38		31,057.53	3,105.75	34,163.29
39		34,163.29	3,416.33	37,579.61
40		37,579.61	3,757.96	41,337.57
41		41,337.57	4,133.76	45,471.33
42		45,471.33	4,547.13	50,018.47
43		50,018.47	5,001.85	55,020.31
44		55,020.31	5,502.03	60,522.34
45		60,522.34	6,052.23	66,574.58
46		66,574.58	6,657.46	73,232.04

(continued)

AGE	THE YEAR'S INVESTMENT, $	BEGINNING-OF-YEAR VALUE, $	INTEREST AT 10%, $	END-OF YEAR-VALUE, $
47		73,232.04	7,323.20	80,555.24
48		80,555.24	8,055.52	88,610.76
49		88,610.76	8,861.08	97,471.84
50		97,471.84	9,747.18	107,219.02
51		107,219.02	10,721.90	117,940.93
52		117,940.93	11,794.09	129,735.02
53		129,735.02	12,973.50	142,708.52
54		142,708.52	14,270.85	156,979.37
55		156,979.37	15,697.94	172,677.31
56		172,677.31	17,267.73	189,945.04
57		189,945.04	18,994.50	208,939.54
58		208,939.54	20,893.95	229,833.50
59		229,833.50	22,983.35	252,816.85
60		252,816.85	25,281.68	278,098.53
61		278,098.53	27,809.85	305,908.39
62		305,908.39	30,590.84	336,499.22
63		336,499.22	33,649.92	370,149.15
64		370,149.15	37,014.91	407,164.06
65		407,164.06	40,716.41	447,880.47
66		447,880.47	44,788.05	492,668.52

commence saving. For an example in contrast, let's consider another new graduate. For whatever reason, this one chooses not to save as our previous graduate did. Instead, this graduate waits 10 years until his career is more developed before dedicating the same $1,000 per year toward retirement. Then he continues to invest $1,000 per year for the rest of

his working career until age 66. Assuming that a 10 percent interest rate can still be achieved every year, how much
would you think this second graduate would have? Every student to whom I've ever posed this question has guessed that
this second graduate would definitely have more money by
far. After all, this second person will have invested a total
of $30,000 over the course of 40 years, $1,000 in each of
years 11 through 40. In actuality though, this second person
would have only $298,126, a full $194,541 less than the first
graduate. (See Table 5-5.) The difference is entirely attribut-
able to the first graduate's decision to get time working in her
money's favor immediately.

I usually ask my students a follow-up question. Assuming that the second graduate maintains the discipline to continue investing $1,000 per year and that interest rates remain
at 10 percent per year forever, how long would they esti-
mate it would take for the second graduate's money to catch
up with the first's? Would it be 50 years? 60 years? 75 years?
None of these would be correct. The correct answer is that
the second graduate will never catch up with the first! That's
right; under the stated conditions, the second graduate will
never have as much money as the first!

Our graduates are not unlike the tortoise and the hare,
except that in our case the first graduate is both tortoise and
hare. She starts out with an early lead, and not only does she
not relinquish it, but she consistently extends it. Table 5-6
shows how far her lead extends into the impossibly long term.

TABLE 5-5

AGE	THE YEAR'S INVESTMENT, $	BEGINNING-OF-YEAR VALUE, $	INTEREST AT 10%, $	END-OF YEAR-VALUE, $
22				
23				
24				
25				
26				
27				
28				
29				
30				
31				
32	1,000.00	1,000.00	100.00	1,100.00
33	1,000.00	2,100.00	210.00	2,310.00
34	1,000.00	3,310.00	331.00	3,641.00
35	1,000.00	4,641.00	464.10	5,105.10
36	1,000.00	6,105.10	610.51	6,715.61
37	1,000.00	7,715.61	771.56	8,487.17
38	1,000.00	9,487.17	948.72	10,435.89
39	1,000.00	11,435.89	1,143.59	12,579.48
40	1,000.00	13,579.48	1,357.95	14,937.42
41	1,000.00	15,937.42	1,593.74	17,531.17
42	1,000.00	18,531.17	1,853.12	20,384.28
43	1,000.00	21,384.28	2,138.43	23,522.71
44	1,000.00	24,522.71	2,452.27	26,974.98
45	1,000.00	27,974.98	2,797.50	30,772.48
46	1,000.00	31,772.48	3,177.25	34,949.73

(continued)

TABLE 5-5 (*Continued*)

AGE	THE YEAR'S INVESTMENT, $	BEGINNING-OF-YEAR VALUE, $	INTEREST AT 10%, $	END-OF YEAR-VALUE, $
47	1,000.00	35,949.73	3,594.97	39,544.70
48	1,000.00	40,544.70	4,054.47	44,599.17
49	1,000.00	45,599.17	4,559.92	50,159.09
50	1,000.00	51,159.09	5,115.91	56,275.00
51	1,000.00	57,275.00	5,727.50	63,002.50
52	1,000.00	64,002.50	6,400.25	70,402.75
53	1,000.00	71,402.75	7,140.27	78,543.02
54	1,000.00	79,543.02	7,954.30	87,497.33
55	1,000.00	88,497.33	8,849.73	97,347.06
56	1,000.00	98,347.06	9,834.71	108,181.77
57	1,000.00	109,181.77	10,918.18	120,099.94
58	1,000.00	121,099.94	12,109.99	133,209.94
59	1,000.00	134,209.94	13,420.99	147,630.93
60	1,000.00	148,630.93	14,863.09	163,494.02
61	1,000.00	164,494.02	16,449.40	180,943.42
62	1,000.00	181,943.42	18,194.34	200,137.77
63	1,000.00	201,137.77	20,113.78	221,251.54
64	1,000.00	222,251.54	22,225.15	244,476.70
65	1,000.00	245,476.70	24,547.67	270,024.37
66	1,000.00	271,024.37	27,102.44	298,126.81

My columns for the first student, who no longer makes any further contributions, are truncated for ease of reading. As we can see, by age 100, the first student's nest egg will have appreciated to over $12 million, while the second student's will be less than $8 million.

I believe the point should be very clear by now. Such is the power of the time value of money that any time lost in the beginning years becomes exponentially more difficult to overcome in later years. The point bears stating again: time truly is money.

TABLE 5-6

FIRST STUDENT		SECOND STUDENT			
AGE	END-OF-YEAR VALUE, $	AGE	THE YEAR'S INVESTMENT, $	BEGINNING-OF-YEAR VALUE, $	INTEREST AT 10%, $	END-OF-YEAR VALUE, $
66	$492,668.52	66	$1,000.00	$271,024.37	$27,102.44	$298,126.81
67	$541,935.37	67	$1,000.00	$299,126.81	$29,912.68	$329,039.49
68	$596,128.90	68	$1,000.00	$330,039.49	$33,003.95	$363,043.43
69	$655,741.79	69	$1,000.00	$364,043.43	$36,404.34	$400,447.78
70	$721,315.97	70	$1,000.00	$401,447.78	$40,144.78	$441,592.56
71	$793,447.57	71	$1,000.00	$442,592.56	$44,259.26	$486,851.81
72	$872,792.33	72	$1,000.00	$487,851.81	$48,785.18	$536,636.99
73	$960,071.56	73	$1,000.00	$537,636.99	$53,763.70	$591,400.69
74	$1,056,078.72	74	$1,000.00	$592,400.69	$59,240.07	$651,640.76
75	$1,161,686.59	75	$1,000.00	$652,640.76	$65,264.08	$717,904.84
76	$1,277,855.25	76	$1,000.00	$718,904.84	$71,890.48	$790,795.32
77	$1,405,640.77	77	$1,000.00	$791,795.32	$79,179.53	$870,974.85
78	$1,546,204.85	78	$1,000.00	$871,974.85	$87,197.49	$959,172.34
79	$1,700,825.33	79	$1,000.00	$960,172.34	$96,017.23	$1,056,189.57
80	$1,870,907.87	80	$1,000.00	$1,057,189.57	$105,718.96	$1,162,908.53
81	$2,057,998.65	81	$1,000.00	$1,163,908.53	$116,390.85	$1,280,299.38
82	$2,263,798.52	82	$1,000.00	$1,281,299.38	$128,129.94	$1,409,429.32
83	$2,490,178.37	83	$1,000.00	$1,410,429.32	$141,042.93	$1,551,472.25
84	$2,739,196.21	84	$1,000.00	$1,552,472.25	$155,247.23	$1,707,719.48
85	$3,013,115.83	85	$1,000.00	$1,708,719.48	$170,871.95	$1,879,591.42

(continued)

TABLE 5-6 (*Continued*)

FIRST STUDENT		SECOND STUDENT				
AGE	END-OF-YEAR VALUE, $	AGE	THE YEAR'S INVESTMENT, $	BEGINNING-OF-YEAR VALUE, $	INTEREST AT 10%, $	END-OF-YEAR VALUE, $
86	$3,314,427.41	86	$1,000.00	$1,880,591.42	$188,059.14	$2,068,650.57
87	$3,645,870.15	87	$1,000.00	$2,069,650.57	$206,965.06	$2,276,615.62
88	$4,010,457.17	88	$1,000.00	$2,277,615.62	$227,761.56	$2,505,377.19
89	$4,411,502.88	89	$1,000.00	$2,506,377.19	$250,637.72	$2,757,014.90
90	$4,852,653.17	90	$1,000.00	$2,758,014.90	$275,801.49	$3,033,816.40
91	$5,337,918.49	91	$1,000.00	$3,034,816.40	$303,481.64	$3,338,298.03
92	$5,871,710.34	92	$1,000.00	$3,339,298.03	$333,929.80	$3,673,227.84
93	$6,458,881.37	93	$1,000.00	$3,674,227.84	$367,422.78	$4,041,650.62
94	$7,104,769.51	94	$1,000.00	$4,042,650.62	$404,265.06	$4,446,915.68
95	$7,815,246.46	95	$1,000.00	$4,447,915.68	$444,791.57	$4,892,707.25
96	$8,596,771.11	96	$1,000.00	$4,893,707.25	$489,370.73	$5,383,077.98
97	$9,456,448.22	97	$1,000.00	$5,384,077.98	$538,407.80	$5,922,485.78
98	$10,402,093.04	98	$1,000.00	$5,923,485.78	$592,348.58	$6,515,834.35
99	$11,442,302.34	99	$1,000.00	$6,516,834.35	$651,683.44	$7,168,517.79
100	$12,586,532.58	100	$1,000.00	$7,169,517.79	$716,951.78	$7,886,469.57

THE 401(K) IMPERATIVE

I wish that I myself had always been fastidious about saving. But I wasn't and had to learn the importance of this lesson the hard way. My hope, however, is that at least my personal experience can be instructive.

For my first job out of college, I moved back to New York City. It was the mid-1980s, and my starting salary was $28,000 at a major financial institution. Even in those years, it was barely enough to live on in the biggest city in the country. Under those conditions, I was not inclined to participate in the bank's 401(k) plan, a common retirement savings program. At the age of 22, any talk about retirement went way over my head. We can already infer from our previous section that this was a big mistake. Only in later years would I realize exactly how big a mistake it was and how much money I had forfeited.

As with most retirement plans, there are two major tax benefits with 401(k) plans. The first is that money invested in a 401(k) plan is not taxed until much later in your life when your income and, therefore, tax bracket would presumably be much lower. This is obviously not the case when making regular purchases. Let's assume that you wish to purchase a candy bar that costs $1.00. How much would you need to earn in order to purchase the candy bar? The answer would be $1.00 only if you paid no tax. But that clearly isn't the case for most people. One must earn somewhat more than $1.00 in order to have $1.00 left to spend. Assume that you're in the 25 percent tax bracket. To calculate the amount that must be earned, the following simple calculation would be required:

Dollar amount divided by (1 minus tax rate)

In our example, that number would be $1.00/(1 − 0.25), which equals $1.33 that must be earned in order to have $1.00 left over to purchase the candy bar.

Now consider how much must be earned in order to purchase $1.00 of investments in a retirement plan like a

401(k). Since money to be invested in a 401(k) plan is not first taxed, purchasing $1.00 of new investments in a 401(k) plan requires one to earn exactly $1.00. This is the first great appeal of investing through 401(k) plans: it "costs" less.

→ Consider the alternative of investing outside of 401(k) plans. The same dollar whittles down to only 75 cents after the 25 percent tax is paid on the dollar. How significant is this difference of just a quarter? We can employ the principle of compound interest once again to determine this. After 44 years of investment at 10 percent, the full dollar within a 401(k) plan will have grown to $72.89. Meanwhile, every dollar that is invested outside of 401(k) protection is first whittled down to 75 cents. As Table 5-7 shows, after 44 years, 75 cents grows to just $54.67, a difference of $18.22.

But actually it gets even more favorable for money invested in a 401(k) plan. This brings us to the second great tax benefit of such plans. Not only is money invested in 401(k) plans not taxed; neither are the gains that the investment achieves. In our previous example, it would not be correct to assume that money outside of a 401(k) plan could grow at the same 10 percent as money inside a 401(k) plan. That's because gains on the funds outside of a 401(k) plan would be taxed every year as the investment grows. Therefore, the 10 percent that the money earns is not a 10 percent gain to you. Actually, it is only 7.5 percent after taxes. The true comparison is $1.00 invested for 44 years at 10 percent versus 75 cents invested for 44 years at 7.5 percent. The final tally now becomes $72.89 versus $21.80, a difference of $51.09. The benefit of the 401(k) plan compared with the outside alternative investment, already great as the result of the first tax advantage, becomes greater still after the second (as can be seen in Table 5-8).

THE MAGNIFICENCE OF THE MATCH

But wait, it gets even better. Employees lucky enough to be able to participate in 401(k) plans frequently find that their employer will match part or all of their personal contributions with company money. This is one of the very few instances in the world of truly free money. A company willing to offer a dollar-for-dollar match has effectively given the employee an instant 100 percent return on his or her money. You could search your whole life and still not be able to find an investor brilliant enough to double your money instantly and without risk. Even the miracle of compound interest pales in comparison to this.

As a result, any employee who has the opportunity to participate in an employer-matched 401(k) plan absolutely must do so. Even if the match is not dollar for dollar, but more commonly, 50 cents for every dollar, the employee must still participate. Once again, no investor, not even the best, could offer you an immediate 50 percent return on your money.

TABLE 5-7

AGE	THE YEAR'S INVESTMENT, $	BEGINNING-OF-YEAR VALUE, $	INTEREST AT 10%, $	END-OF YEAR-VALUE, $
22	1.00	1.00	010	1.10
23		1.10	0.11	1.21
24		1.21	0.12	1.33
25		1.33	0.13	1.46
26		1.46	0.15	1.61
27		1.61	0.16	1.77
28		1.77	018	1.95
29		1.95	0.19	2.14
30		2.14	0..21	2.36
31		2.36	0.24	2.59
32		2.59	026	2.85
33		2.85	0.29	3.14
34		3.14	0.31	3.45
35		3.45	0.35	3.80
36		3.80	0.38	4.18
37		4.18	0.42	4.59
38		4.59	0.46	5.05
39		5.05	0.51	5.56
40		5.56	0.56	6.12
41		6.12	0.61	6.73
42		6.73	0.67	7.40
43		7.40	0.74	8.14
44		8.14	0.81	8.95
45		8.95	0.90	9.85
46		9.85	0.98	10.83

(continued)

AGE	THE YEAR'S INVESTMENT, $	BEGINNING-OF-YEAR VALUE, $	INTEREST AT 10%, $	END-OF YEAR-VALUE, $
47		10.83	1.08	11.92
48		11.92	1.19	13.11
49		13.11	1.31	14.42
50		14.42	1.44	15.86
51		15.86	1.59	17.45
52		17.45	1.74	19.19
53		1919	1.92	21.11
54		21.11	2.11	23.23
55		23.23	2.32	25.55
56		25.55	2.55	28.10
57		28.10	2.81	30.91
58		30.91	3.09	34.00
59		34.00	3.40	37.40
60		37.40	3.74	41.14
61		41.14	4.11	45.26
62		45.26	4.53	49.79
63		49.79	4.98	54.76
64		54.76	5.48	60.24
65		60.24	6.02	66.26
66		66.26	6.63	72.89

(continued)

TABLE 5-7 *(Continued)*

AGE	THE YEAR'S INVESTMENT, $	BEGINNING-OF-YEAR VALUE, $	INTEREST AT 10%, $	END-OF YEAR-VALUE, $
22	0.75	0.75	0.08	0.83
23		0.83	0.08	0.91
24		0.91	0,09	1.00
25		1.00	0 10	1.10
26		1.10	0.11	121
27		1.21	0.12	1.33
28		1.33	0.13	1.46
29		1.46	0.15	1.61
30		1.61	0.16	1.77
31		1.77	0.18	1.95
32		1.95	0.19	2.14
33		2.14	0.21	2.35
34		2.35	0.24	2.59
35		2.59	0.26	2.85
36		2.85	0.28	3.13
37		3.13	0.31	3.45
38		3.45	0.34	3.79
39		3.79	0.38	4.17
40		4.17	0.42	4.59
41		4.59	0.46	5.05
42		5.05	0.50	5.55
43		5.55	0.56	6.11
44		6.11	0.61	6.72
45		6.72	0.67	739
46		7.39	0.74	8.13

(continued)

AGE	THE YEAR'S INVESTMENT, $	BEGINNING-OF- YEAR VALUE, $	INTEREST AT 10%, $	END-OF YEAR-VALUE, $
47		8.13	0.81	8.94
48		8.94	0.89	9.83
49		9.83	0.98	10.82
50		10.82	1.08	11.90
51		11.90	1.19	13.09
52		13.09	1.31	14.40
53		14.40	1.44	15.84
54		15.84	1.58	17.42
55		17.42	1.74	19.16
56		19.16	1.92	2108
57		21.08	2.11	23.18
58		23.18	2.32	25.50
59		25.50	2.55	28.05
60		28.05	2.81	30.86
61		30.86	309	33.94
62		33.94	3.39	37.34
63		37.34	3.73	41.07
64		4107	4.11	45.18
65		45.18	4.52	49.70
66		49.70	4.97	54.67

TABLE 5-8

AGE	THE YEAR'S INVESTMENT, $	BEGINNING-OF-YEAR VALUE, $	INTEREST AT 10%, $	END-OF YEAR-VALUE, $
22	1.00	1.00	0.10	1.10
23		1.10	0.11	1.21
24		1.21	0.12	1.33
25		1.33	0.13	1.46
26		1.46	0.15	1.61
27		1.61	0.16	1.77
28		1.77	0.18	1.95
29		1.95	0.19	2.14
30		2.14	0.21	2.36
31		2.36	0.24	2.59
32		2.59	0.26	2.85
33		2.85	0.29	3.14
34		3.14	0.31	3.45
35		3.45	0.35	380
36		3.80	0.38	4.18
37		4.18	0.42	4.59
38		4.59	0.46	5.05
39		5.05	0.51	5.56
40		5.56	0.56	6.12
41		6 12	0.61	6.73
42		6.73	0.67	7.40
43		7.40	0.74	8.14
44		8 14	0.81	8.95
45		8.95	0.90	9.85
46		9.85	0.98	10.83

(continued)

AGE	THE YEAR'S INVESTMENT, $	BEGINNING-OF-YEAR VALUE, $	INTEREST AT 10%, $	END-OF YEAR-VALUE, $
47		10.83	1.08	11.92
48		11.92	1.19	13.11
49		13.11	1.31	14.42
50		14.42	1.44	15.86
51		15.86	1.59	17.45
52		17.45	1.74	19.19
53		19.19	1.92	21.11
54		21.11	2.11	23.23
55		23.23	2.32	25.55
56		25.55	2.55	28.10
57		28.10	2.81	30.91
58		30.91	3.09	34.00
59		34.00	3.40	37.40
60		37.40	3.74	41.14
61		41.14	4.11	45.26
62		45.26	453	49.79
63		49.79	498	54.76
64		54.76	5.48	60.24
65		60.24	6.02	66.26
66		66.26	6.63	72.89

(continued)

TABLE 5-8 *(Continued)*

AGE	THE YEAR'S INVESTMENT, $	BEGINNING-OF-YEAR VALUE, $	INTEREST AT 10%, $	END-OF YEAR-VALUE, $
22	0.75	0.75	0.06	0.81
23		0.81	0.06	0.87
24		0.87	0.07	0.93
25		0.93	0.07	1.00
26		1.00	0.08	1.08
27		1.08	0.08	1.16
28		1.16	0.09	1.24
29		1.24	0.09	1.34
30		1.34	0.10	1.44
31		1.44	0.11	1.55
32		1.55	0.12	1.66
33		1.66	0.12	1.79
34		1.79	0.13	1.92
35		1.92	0.14	2.06
36		2.06	0.15	2.22
37		2.22	0.17	2.39
38		2.39	0.18	2.56
39		2.56	0.19	2.76
40		2.76	0.21	2.96
41		2.96	0.22	3.19
42		3.19	0.24	3.42
43		3.42	0.26	3.68
44		3.68	0.28	3.96
45		3.96	0.30	4.25
46		4.25	0.32	4.57

(continued)

AGE	THE YEAR'S INVESTMENT, $	BEGINNING-OF-YEAR VALUE, $	INTEREST AT 10%, $	END-OF YEAR-VALUE, $
47		4.57	0.34	4.92
48		4.92	0.37	5.29
49		5.29	0.40	5.68
50		5.68	0.43	6.11
51		6.11	0.46	6.57
52		6.57	0.49	706
53		706	0.53	7.59
54		7.59	0.57	816
55		816	0.61	8.77
56		8.77	0.66	9.43
57		9.43	0.71	10.13
58		10.13	0.76	10.89
59		10.89	0.82	11.71
60		11.71	0.88	12.59
61		12.59	094	13.53
62		13.53	1.01	14.89
63		14.89	1.12	16.38
64		16.38	1.23	18.01
65		18.01	1.35	19.81
66		19.81	1.49	21.80

Let's return to my personal example. I worked at that financial institution for 4 years and had the opportunity to participate in the 401(k) plan the entire time. As it happened, my first employer was particularly generous with its plan. This is unheard of now, but that employer was actually willing to match $2.00 for every $1.00 any employee put into the plan. That would have been an immediate 200 percent return on investment!

Now we can start to appreciate what I truly gave up by not participating. Nominally, I lost "only" $2,000 for every $1,000 I did not invest in each of my 4 years there. That's bad enough. But I also gave up the accumulated benefit of 40 years of tax-free investment. In total, what I forfeited after 44 years of compound growth at 10 percent was, as Table 5-9 shows, $762,474.98. This would have come from an investment of my own money of only $4,000! I might hit the pavement if I dwelled long on this number.

IRAs

People not lucky enough to be able to participate in 401(k) plans have the next best thing in individual retirement accounts (IRAs). The key word is *individual*. You must establish them yourself with a financial institution. Necessarily though, this means that you will not have the benefit of an employer match. That's unfortunate, but IRAs are still the most valuable savings vehicle for anyone without access to a

401(k) plan. In fact, they are very valuable even if someone does have access to a 401(k) plan. After reaching their limit on 401(k) plans, people with the ability to do so should consider investing in an IRA because there's really no such thing as saving too much.

The specific numbers change annually, but in general, IRAs permit people below a certain income to invest up to $5,000 per year ($6,000 if you're 50 or older) into these self-directed funds. This amount is then deductible from federal taxes, just as with 401(k) plans. Also, just as with 401(k) plans, the gains that the investment earns are permitted to compound tax-free. These two benefits, even though there is no possibility of a company match, make an IRA the next best savings vehicle.

ROTH IRAs

Following behind IRAs in importance for the hypersaver are the newer Roth IRAs. These vehicles do not have the benefit of the employer match and also do not permit the tax deductibility of the investment. You might therefore wonder what makes them so special. The answer is that with Roth IRAs, one still has the benefit of tax-free compounding.

This benefit alone can mean the difference between a comfortable versus a lavish retirement. As we saw from a previous discussion, this benefit is still considerable. Consider the future value of $50,000 invested for 44 years at 7.5 per-

TABLE 5-9

AGE	MY INVESTMENT, $	COMPANY MATCH, $	BEGINNING-OF-YEAR VALUE, $	INTEREST AT 10%, $	END-OF YEAR-VALUE, $
22	1,000.00	2,000.00	3,000.00	300.00	3,300.00
23	1,000.00	2,000.00	6,300.00	630.00	6,930.00
24	1,000.00	2,000.00	9,930.00	993.00	10,923.00
25	1,000.00	2,000.00	13,923.00	1,392.30	15,315.30
26			15,315.30	1,531.53	16,846.83
27			16,846.83	1,684.68	18,531.51
28			18,531.51	1,853.15	20,384.66
29			20,384.66	2,038.47	22,423.13
30			22,423.13	2,242.31	24,665.44
31			24,665.44	2,466.54	27,131.99
32			27,131.99	2,713.20	29,845.19
33			29,845.19	2,984.52	32,829.71
34			32,829.71	3,282.97	36,112.68
35			36,112.68	3,611.27	39,723.94
36			39,723.94	3,972.39	43,696.34
37			43,696.34	4,369.63	48,065.97
38			48,065.97	4,806.60	52,872.57
39			52,872.57	5,287.26	58,159.83
40			58,159.83	5,815.98	63,975.81
41			63,975.81	6,397.58	70,373.39
42			70,373.39	7,037.34	77,410.73
43			77,410.73	7,741.07	85,151.80
44			85,151.80	8,515.18	93,666.98
45			93,666.98	9,366.70	103,033.68
46			103,033.68	10,303.37	113,337.05

(continued)

AGE	MY INVESTMENT, $	COMPANY MATCH, $	BEGINNING-OF-YEAR VALUE, $	INTEREST AT 10%, $	END-OF YEAR-VALUE, $
47			113,337.05	11,333.70	124,670.75
48			124,670.75	12,467.08	137,137.83
49			137,137.83	13,713.78	150,851.61
50			150,851.61	15,085.16	165,936.77
51			165,936.77	16,593.68	182,530.45
52			182,530.45	18,253.04	200,783.49
53			200,783.49	20,078.35	220,861.84
54			220,861.84	22,086.18	242,948.03
55			242,948.03	24,294.80	267,242.83
56			267,242.83	26,724.28	293,967.11
57			293,967.11	29,396.71	323,363.82
58			323,363.82	32,336.38	355,700.21
59			355,700.21	35,570.02	391,270.23
60			391,270.23	39,127.02	430,397.25
61			430,397.25	43,039.73	473,436.98
62			473,436.98	47,343.70	520,780.67
63			520,780.67	52,078.07	572,858.74
64			572,858.74	57,285.87	630,144.62
65			630,144.62	63,014.46	693,159.08
66			693,159.08	69,315.91	762,474.98

cent versus the same $50,000 invested for 44 years at 10 percent. The first represents investing outside of a Roth IRA and the second within one. The first yields $1.2 million, but the second yields more than twice that much, $3.3 million. I rest my case.

529s

529 plans come next. For these vehicles, there is no match, and there no is tax deduction, and even the use of the funds is limited. However, for people who have college educations rather than retirement to fund, 529 plans are a godsend. Like 401(k) plans, the number 529 refers to the part of the tax code which gave rise to this investment. And its rise has been truly meteoric. From its inception in 2000, money invested in 529 plans grew to over $140 billion by 2011.

Just as with 401(k) plans, IRAs, and Roth IRAs, the miracle of tax-free compound interest is the key draw. However, there's a cruel caveat. If the investor's child chooses not to attend college, there are severe penalties. Money withdrawn for any purpose other than education expenses will be cruelly punished. The investment gains, which had been tax-advantaged for so long, would be subject to income tax plus a penalty. This is quite drastic, and therefore one should think very carefully about one's college plans before undertaking a 529 plan.

FIRST FRUITS

I hope by now it's clear how important it is to begin saving as much and as early as possible. Most financial advisors recommend setting aside 10 percent of every paycheck at a minimum. I agree. With apologies to theologians, I call this the first fruits principle. Behavioral economists confirm a very simple underlying concept: what you don't see, you won't miss. Therefore, what you want to make invisible is that first 10 percent. This is easiest to do with an employer's 401(k) plan, but if you don't have access to one, automatic debiting from your paycheck into your bank account makes this very easy. Doing just this removes the temptation to skip any paycheck's contribution. With the first fruits principle, individuals can eventually accumulate their own million dollars. Prove it for yourself.

SOW EARLY; SOW OFTEN

Frugality has been a custom and a virtue of the Chinese for generations, serving them very well in country after country. It is a lesson for modern America that should be heeded. Especially with the availability of tax-advantaged tools like IRAs, 401(k)s, and 529s, there is no excuse for anyone not to save. Just apply the first fruits principle. It works like magic.

SUMMARY

What is the key lesson in this chapter? It breaks down into four parts:

1. Sow early; sow often. The more money you sow in the early years, the more you'll reap in later years.

2. Utilize the advantages permitted in the tax code to help more of your money work for you. No one should ignore the tax benefits of investing within retirement plans.

3. Obtain company matching funds if at all possible. This is truly a great gift from many employers.

4. Let time and the miracle of compound interest do your heavy lifting for you.

It's as simple as that. This is the fifth principle of the Chinese Way to Wealth and Prosperity.

CHAPTER SIX

DEFER GRATIFICATION

Everyone has surely heard the saying commonly attributed to philosopher Lao Tzu, "A journey of a thousand miles must begin with a single step." People usually use this expression as encouragement for starting any demanding task. However, there's another context used less often which places the emphasis on the thousand miles rather than on the single step. In so doing, it articulates the Chinese focus on the long term. This has many financial manifestations, from earning to saving to investing and even to career management. Such a focus on the very long term, sometimes beyond one's own lifetime, and ignoring the lure of immediate or intermediate gratification, is a form of human capital that the Chinese have in great abundance.

STANFORD AND THE IROQUOIS

In 1972, a famous experiment was conducted at Stanford University involving, of all things, marshmallows. A group of four-year-olds was offered one marshmallow to eat immediately or two marshmallows if they were willing to wait 20 minutes. Purely as an economic experiment, the 20-minute wait would seem more than worthwhile for double the reward.

But this was not an economic experiment. It was a psychological one. These children were tracked into their adolescence to measure their emotional and intellectual development. After the data were collected and analyzed, it was concluded that the children who were able to delay gratification, that is, those who waited the 20 minutes for two marshmallows, ultimately developed into better adjusted, more dependable people. They also had fewer behavioral problems, struggled less in stressful situations, and scored on average 210 points higher on the Scholastic Aptitude Test. On average, the patient group even had a significantly lower body-mass index.

The results of this experiment are frequently used to emphasize the importance of deferring gratification. It is the ability to defer gratification that enables one to take the long view in economics and personal finance. Chinese people are always taking the long view.

Of course, 20 minutes does not constitute any particularly long period of time. In fact, 20 minutes means next to nothing economically. But as we saw in Chapter 5, the time-value-of-money concept over the longer term is a mathematical miracle. The key question is, do we have the fortitude to delay gratification for the duration of the long run to give our money time to work in our favor?

The idea of taking the long view is encapsulated in a principle known as the *seven-generation view*. Credit must be given to the Iroquois for promulgating it in America. According to the Great Law of the Iroquois from the Constitution of the Iroquois Nations, "In every deliberation, we must consider the impact on the seventh generation." This great law holds that it is necessary to plan seven generations ahead in making decisions. I seem to hear it most often these days in discussions of environmentalism, as proponents debate the effect of policies 200 years into the future.

But in my childhood, I had heard the same thing from my grandmother, who, never having had the luxury of an education, could not possibly have known the Iroquois saying. As memory serves, she was making a point about genealogy and the importance of maintaining the memory of ancestors from seven generations back. Then she took the principle forward and spoke of the importance of our own legacy seven generations into the future on all matters, although I principally took it to mean the securing of prosperity for one's offspring.

At least in the Chinese context, it probably couldn't be taken literally. Seven generations would be the distance from ourselves to our great-great-great-great-grandparents. In my family, I somehow doubt that my own great-great-great-great-grandparents had my welfare in mind. But I believe the principle is clear.

Combining Lao Tzu's proverb with this principle gives us a very important manifestation of Chinese human capital. It is indeed necessary to plan for the seventh generation; therefore, start now. The Chinese have done it this way for centuries.

GOING DEEP

The value of this critical facet of human capital was made crystal clear to me when later in life I had the tremendous privilege of studying with Dr. Martin Seligman, director of the Positive Psychology Center at the University of Pennsylvania and founder of the discipline of positive psychology. I had the distinct pleasure to be admitted into the first master class he conducted to train coaches in his certified Authentic Happiness curriculum.

We learned many tools from him, but one is particularly relevant to this chapter. We learned about the crucial difference between pleasures, which are ephemeral, and abiding happiness, which is magnificently deeper. Countless generations of Chinese parents have had a strong intuitive understanding of this difference.

Pleasure and happiness are not the same thing, although colloquial usage often conflates the two. For instance, Merriam-Webster Online (http: www.merriam-webster.com/dictionary/happiness) offers the following as a secondary definition of the word *happiness*: "pleasurable or satisfying experience." This would suggest that to Webster's, happiness and pleasure are indistinguishable.

But Dr. Seligman delineated differently. Paraphrasing his redefinitions in my own words, pleasure would be a positive tickling of the senses with little lasting effect. Tasting ice cream, watching an exciting movie, taking thrilling vacations—these are all quite gratifying pleasures. But they do not define happiness, nor do they even necessarily lead to it. After the enjoyment of the moment has passed, there is no emotional remnant of the experience. Psychologists use the term *hedonic treadmill* to describe a life lived in pursuit of such pleasures. Since pleasure from such experiences dissipates rather quickly, a life lived in pursuit of them quickly becomes a treadmill existence wherein no progress is actually made toward the goal of obtaining happiness, despite strenuous effort.

In contrast, happiness is a longer-term state of well-being and contentment. As with many other things in life, the critical difference is in the timing. Happiness is unlikely to result quickly. Dr. Seligman's definition is borrowed from Aristotle's *Nicomachean Ethics*. The philosopher Aristotle used the term *eudemonia* to describe the highest state of human emotion. It includes doing good and living well but transcends both. The later coinage of the term *self-actualization* as the realization of one's full potential comes close. Unlike pleasure, this state cannot be achieved in the short term.

In fact, the pursuits of pleasure and happiness are not only uncorrelated; they might work against each other. It's relatively easy to see how the hedonic life would not lead to happiness. Guilty pleasures are prime examples. The consumption of fast food or nicotine or alcohol could not lead to a self-actualized life. The self-actualized life may result despite such consumption but would not result because of it.

One big step worse than guilty pleasures is addictions, which completely negate the possibility of ever achieving happiness. The drug addict, the nicotine addict, the alcoholic, etc., presumably get some form of sensory pleasure from indulging their addiction. But their very indulgence ruins the chance to achieve their highest potential.

However, even as the pleasure seeker will likely not achieve happiness, it must be admitted that the "happy" or "self-actualized" person might not actually experience much pleasure. Consider one's choice of spending an evening either navigating through great works of literature or sitting through reruns of television sit-coms. The latter presumably would be pleasurable. At best, the shenanigans of sit-com characters offer some light entertainment and, the hope is, a diversion from the travails of the day. But there is no lasting effect from spending one's time this way. Thus, there is pleasure but no abiding happiness.

In contrast, consider the demands of making your way through Tolstoy. I believe this would not be pleasurable for most of us. My own experience with Tolstoy in high school was definitely not pleasurable (nor was anything else I studied in high school). In any case, plowing through the classics requires diligence and perseverance. There's an unattributed saying I heard in college that a classic is a book that one wishes to have read but one does not wish to read.

However, consider the achievement of having spent a lifetime of evenings working through the greatest works of literature, works by Shakespeare, Tolstoy, Dostoyevsky, Hemmingway, Joyce, and Proust. The intellectual gains would be tremendous. An abiding happiness would result, as there would from the accomplishment of any major achievement.

Knowing this explains Chinese parents' particular insistence that their children spend their spare time studying the piano, or chess, or calligraphy, or indeed anything. For most children, there is little or no pleasure involved. (Nor, frankly, is there for the parents.) But the long-term benefits that result from their children knowing how to play a Mozart sonata or unravel an intractable problem are immeasurable. That is authentic happiness.

There is an athletic analogy, too. Presumably even Michael Phelps does not enjoy waking up at five o'clock in the morning in the freezing cold of a typical Baltimore winter to be dragged through yet another grueling Olympic work-out by his coach. Most of us couldn't even handle the waking-up part, let alone the working-out part. There couldn't be any pleasure in this. But consider the young man's happiness from having won (at the time of this writing) 14 Olympic gold medals.

There is direct relevance for all the rest of us who are not gifted with Olympic-caliber talent. The term *feel the burn* has proliferated throughout the country's gyms and health clubs for a reason. The burn spoken of is the pain of lifting the additional 10 pounds or of running the final mile. That wouldn't be anyone's definition of pleasure. But it can be part of everyone's definition of happiness. This link to happiness is the fuel that propels us through the burn we feel.

From the perspective of personal finance, indulgence in personal pleasure can be the very death of prosperity. Plea-sures can be found, but they rarely come cheaply, as any addict knows. Quite apart from the expense of the indulgence itself, there is also financial "death" in the loss of time. This has two separate financial dimensions. Money spent indulg-ing cannot be invested for the long term. Time spent indulging cannot be utilized learning proper personal finance.

Sigmund Freud described the pleasure principle as the human need to seek pleasure and avoid forms of suffering. This would be the world we wish we could make. He also described an alternate principle, the reality principle. As its name might suggest, this is the world that we would not have chosen to make but one that we are bequeathed nevertheless. In the reality principle, one has accepted the greater long-term good in deferring immediate pleasures. For Chinese mothers, with their eyes ever focused on their children's futures, the choice between the pleasure principle and the reality principle is no choice at all.

THE POWER OF MINDFULNESS

The true puzzlement is why we in the United States seem to have lost sight of the reality principle. Surely the country that has more MBAs and schools of business than any other country should not need to be reminded. In business schools, across all subjects, students are taught relevant skills in business planning. In these courses, all sorts of qualitative and quantitative skills are taught to prepare students for just the sort of long-term planning that businesses require.

I'll be the first to admit that we in the business school professoriate fully expect some students to forget completely much of what we teach. I assume this is the case in any discipline. But long-term planning wouldn't seem to be among the forgotten.

There's an unattributed Chinese proverb that "you should dig a well before you are thirsty." Secretary of State Hillary Clinton used it herself in her 2009 visit to Beijing. I'm sure the meaning is obvious enough to anyone. I'm also sure that many cultures have some similar proverb urging early action. "A stitch in time saves nine" and "the early bird catches the worm" are examples in English that allude to the importance of planning early.

But as memorable as they are, these aphorisms haven't taken hold in practice in the West, as the Chinese one has in the East. I believe the reason is that the Chinese and the other East Asian cultures have a particular focus on mindfulness. This requires a bit of explanatory background.

Far below the radar of most Americans, Buddhism has become the fastest-growing religion in the country. In recent decades, while most other religions have been experiencing declining membership, Buddhism has grown its ranks several times over. In 2008, the Pew Research Center reported that Buddhism had overtaken Islam for third place behind only Christianity and Judaism in total number of adherents in the United States.

Buddhism is no longer all that foreign to most Americans. That is because the extraordinary popularity of yoga in recent years has spurred at least a passing familiarity with Buddhism. The Chinese have an ancient system of yoga too. Known as Taoist yoga, it has made strides in the West along with the other schools of yoga.

Just as there are many schools of yoga, so are there many schools of Buddhism. Like Protestantism, the underlying philosophy of the different schools of Buddhism, known as the Dharma, is basically the same. Also basically the same in all forms of Buddhism is their emphasis on meditation. In much of East Asia, the practice of meditation has transcended the Buddhist religion itself, so that many non-Buddhists (including me) practice meditation for its myriad benefits.

Technically, what we are practicing is not meditation per se. Meditation is only the vehicle. The goal of meditation is mindfulness. Although defining mindfulness directly is challenging, it is very easy to understand when contrasted with its antonym, mindlessness.

Those who work mindlessly are not being diligent. Those who study mindlessly are not concentrating. Those who live mindlessly are wasting their lives. Therefore, developing the skill of mindfulness is an attempt to become more fully alive in all areas.

This is commonly misunderstood. In fact, much about Buddhism is commonly misunderstood. People see Buddhists meditating and think they're trying to zone out. That is exactly the opposite of what they're doing. A proper meditation session leaves one more aware and thus more mindful of his or her life, surroundings, and emotions.

Method actors of the Stanislavski school have a term called being in the moment, which I believe is relevant. An actor who is truly in the moment when performing is not just playing the role of a character. This actor becomes the character. It is similar to someone who has learned to be fully mindful. In this case, the person is being in the moment with his or her own life.

Being mindful and in the moment are quite different from and in fact are diametrically opposite of the similar-sounding philosophy to live like there's no tomorrow. The latter is a hedonist philosophy giving no heed to the consequences of today's actions. Being mindful, on the other hand, accepts the responsibility of the tomorrows while appreciating the beauty of the todays. This full mindfulness is what Chinese culture via Buddhism has imparted.

Meditating to achieve mindfulness is not easy. It isn't usually fun. It requires a great, great deal of patience. But the need to build patience, even if one cannot achieve it personally, is something that Chinese parents have drilled into their children for centuries. Patience is the singular ingredient in the Stanford experiment which separated the life winners from the runners-up.

The medical evidence produced in recent decades by doctors and scientists is incontrovertible. There are few things better for alleviating the modern epidemic of anxiety than meditation. But the benefits go far beyond the alleviation of hypertension. Like studying, the doing is frequently not enjoyable. There is little pleasure involved. But the gratification that comes later is permanent.

SEINFELD VERSUS FRASIER

I believe a flippant illustration can be drawn with some familiar fictional characters. Notwithstanding what I previously wrote about the futility of watching sit-coms, I was quite a fan of the show *Frasier*. Watching television is not something I do often, and so I must really love what I'm watching to spend time doing it. I did. As the show hit its stride, it was moved to the prime Thursday night slot formerly occupied by *Seinfeld*. I think the two Thursday night shows illustrate my point quite whimsically.

Seinfeld was a show about nothing. It was proud of that. There was only a minimal plotline in most episodes. Much of the show consisted of the characters ruminating, albeit hilariously, about this or that observation about life. One could well wonder (to the extent one should ever wonder about fictitious characters) how these people had so much free time on their hands. The show's finale ended with the principal characters languishing in jail.

Frasier, in contrast, had rather impressive story lines. The characters were fully fleshed out, and the occupations of the principal characters were vital components of most episodes' story lines. Frasier himself, despite a number of character flaws quite common to men, was fully engaged in his occupation. He loved it. In one string of episodes, his coping with the loss of employment provided the hilarious backstory. In this show's concluding episode, Frasier prepares enthusiastically to embark upon an exciting new journey.

My analogy is admittedly tenuous. But I still believe the point is valid. The fully engaged life is the one that is worth living and that is conducive to happiness. It is no coincidence that Frasier occupied high societal status as a psychiatrist and lived well as a result. Seinfeld made a threadbare living as a comedian. Seinfeld's was the life of the hedonic treadmill. Frasier came far closer to eudemonia. No Chinese parents wish for their children the achievement of Jerry Seinfeld's character in the show. But all Chinese parents wish for their children the professional achievements of Frasier Crane.

CONFUCIAN DYNAMISM

In the 1980s, a social psychologist from Stanford University named Michael Harris Bond conducted a landmark study of the Chinese psyche. His end product was called the Chinese Values Survey. As its name might suggest, the study was intended to ascertain on what dimensions the Chinese differ most from other people in the world. The initial survey was given to a statistically valid sampling of people from 23 countries.

The results were surprising only in the depth of the conclusions. In a nutshell, the survey determined that the Chinese people differed most from other people in the world in the extent of their long-term orientation, something Dr. Bond called "Confucian dynamism."

On this factor, in first place by a long shot was China. In second and third place were Hong Kong and Taiwan, respectively. Also relevant is that Japan and South Korea finished in fourth and fifth place, respectively, giving the Confucian-oriented cultures a clean sweep in the long-term orientation Olympics. (The United States finished seventeenth, six places from the bottom.)

In naming this long-term orientation *Confucian dynamism*, Dr. Bond gave credit to the philosopher for inculcating an entire litany of virtues that together form a culture's long-term outlook. The results were subsequently used by fellow social psychologist Geert Hofstede to explain the economic success of these countries. Although Confucian dynamism does not work in isolation to explain those successes, it is nevertheless a critical, probably the most critical, variable in the explanatory process.

This is not difficult to understand. The degree to which a society embraces the value of long-term commitments to anything certainly speaks well for that society's eventual success. This works for corporate as well as for individual commitments. The professors Hofstede and Bond were far from alone in isolating the common variable in the success of these East Asian countries. Futurist Herman Kahn had done so famously in the late 1970s in predicting the rise of these same countries. Kahn had presciently determined that the neo-Confucian basis of these countries' cultures would make them a tremendous economic force.

It would be well beyond the scope of this chapter to discuss why the West in general and the United States in particular cannot seem to develop a longer-term orientation. I would submit that we used to have it in the United States. Certainly, our Founding Fathers knew something about sacrifice and dedication to a cause. They were willing to literally risk their lives, their fortunes, and their sacred reputations to fight for a cause they felt was just and in their country's best interest. Now that's long-term orientation.

But at some point in the two-and-a-quarter centuries since the American Revolution, we seem to have misplaced this great virtue. Since well before the global economic crisis began, it had become commonplace to the point of trite to criticize the short-term profit focus of our corporation leaders. It has similarly been common to bemoan our youngsters' lack of dedication and focus.

Criticizing and bemoaning will only take us so far though. Just as one cannot dethrone a boxing champion without a title fight, one cannot simply wish away an ineffective orientation. It requires replacement by a better, more efficacious one. I hope and think we are on the cusp of doing so in the United States.

SUMMARY

The perils of America's continuing obsession with the moment are almost too dire to consider. But if we don't, we won't stand a chance of competing with countries that actually do focus on the long term.

I do not in any way suggest that America turn to a full austerity model. I seriously doubt the efficacy of any economic policy that takes away a citizenry's desire to work. The failure of communism determined this definitively.

Instead, I believe that the teaching of values be returned front and center to the family dinner table. Values can be taught elsewhere in society, but no unit is more responsible for imparting values than one's own parents. We have much work to do. Perhaps some of us are already doing this work. In that case, it only requires some tweaking. But in all cases, greater attention must be paid to the necessity, even joy, of deferring gratification.

I do not believe that deferring gratification need be torturous. As mentioned previously, no competitive athlete would want to be relieved of the pain of training. As Buddhists teach us about life in general, pain is inevitable, but suffering is not. It is that way with athletes in training. It is that way with intellectuals in studying. It is that way with tradespeople in serving apprenticeships. And it could be that way with Americans in focusing.

When I was younger, I could not see any pleasure in postponing the enjoyment of spending my hard-earned dollars. However, as I got older, I began to see the wisdom of my parents' teaching about saving for a rainy day. Sometime after that, I did indeed feel pleasure from seeing my investment accounts rise in value, first from my contributions, then later from their own growth.

If there is a silver lining to be found, there might be one in China's own nascent struggle to curb consumerism among its young. Something about misery loving company comes to mind as I write this. Perhaps it's just a global symptom of youth to desire more than they can afford. Perhaps it's another symptom of youth to plan primarily for the moment. Be that as it may, China is already experiencing some of the pains that bedevil the United States. We could call this a pleasant problem, but it is a problem nevertheless.

The pleasant part is that it couldn't have happened to this extent without a burgeoning middle class. The problem part is that a continuation of the trend could eventually cause the very collapse of that same middle class. Haven't we heard fears about the impending demise of the American middle class for decades?

The sacrifices and wisdom of previous generations in any country must be revered. This would first necessitate learning about them. Then slowly we must learn to emulate at least some of the will our ancestors had.

If we can achieve this, we would have discovered more than another principle in the Chinese Way to Wealth and Prosperity. We would achieve true prosperity in all aspects of our lives.

CHAPTER SEVEN

LOVE THE LAND

Novelist Pearl S. Buck knew the Chinese people very well. The daughter of American missionaries, she grew up in China during particularly tumultuous years in the early twentieth century. Although China has been rife with turmoil throughout its history, the wholesale demise of the dynastic system made life particularly challenging in China during the years of Pearl Buck's early youth. Foreigners like her, never especially welcome in China, had special challenges during this time. But she and her family were of hardy stock and would not leave. Though not Chinese, she knew only China as her home. And she loved it.

As conditions worsened, she had the right that every American citizen has to return to the United States. But she resisted and only saw the United States for the first time when it was time for her to attend college. However, such was her affinity for the Chinese people that, after completing her degree, she along with her new husband would return to China. Her husband was an agronomist and therefore was very comfortable in the countryside. This was important, because the couple would not ensconce themselves in the foreign settlements of the large cities. Instead, they moved inland to live among Chinese farmers.

It was these people and their lives that inspired her to write her classic trilogy about China. The best known of these, *The Good Earth*, would win her the Pulitzer Prize in 1932.

In this book, she tells the story of the impoverished Wang family's rise to wealth. Those who have read the book know that the title expresses the moral of the story quite succinctly. Although the fortunes of any family can wax and wane, the earth is good, real estate is wealth, and land is the only source of peace and security. Far more important than detailing particulars about the prototypical family's life, Pearl Buck did a magnificent job in presenting something unique in the Chinese soul about owning property. This forms the next principle in the Chinese path to prosperity.

"THEY'RE NOT MAKING IT ANYMORE"

When asked for investment advice, Mark Twain, the great American humorist, reportedly advised his questioner to buy land because they're not making it anymore. Trenchant as always, Twain provides as good an investment rationale for land as any modern strategist could.

Twain, like any good economist would, zeroes in on the fundamental variable in the valuation of a good: its scarcity. The scarcer something is, the more valuable it becomes. What it can be used for is only of secondary importance. Something as inert as gold has always been the most highly prized holding in the world, but it actually has relatively very few intrinsic uses. The "consumption" of gold for jewelry and industrial purposes is rather small, but this doesn't detract from the appeal of the yellow metal because it is so scarce.

And as Twain noted, land is also scarce. However, simple scarcity wouldn't explain the Chinese affinity for it. Land is scarce in any country. What is so prominent about land in China is a particular cultural constraint against parting with it.

Much more so than in other cultures, the Chinese do not view land as just another asset in an investment portfolio. First, unlike gold, land has tremendous intrinsic use, primarily for agriculture. Thus, to sell land is tantamount to selling your family's food supply. For a country in which food has always been hard to obtain, it becomes nearly heretical to sell the family land. Necessarily, this makes the supply of land for sale very limited.

But beyond this utilitarian function, land has another, deeper appeal to the Chinese. The same Confucian culture that so reveres family and ancestry also places a high degree of reverence on the family home. However modest the property may be, one's home actually is one's castle, and it would be anathema to part with it since it provides more security than anything else in feudal China could. Even under conditions of famine, a family would pawn the family jewels and starve to the brink of death before parting with the family estate. Pearl Buck accurately illustrates this in *The Good Earth*.

With such a dynamic at play, it can be of no surprise that, historically, turnover of real estate would be minimal. A landed family would likely remain landed, and the unlanded would have little opportunity to obtain land.

But times change even though cultural attitudes do not. Just as a child most desires the very toy he or she cannot have, after centuries of acculturation, the Chinese psyche hungers to acquire land at any and every opportunity. As a result, China's opening has unleashed a torrent of Chinese on a veritable shopping spree around the world.

KIDS IN A CANDY STORE

In the final few years of the twentieth century, a mania of sorts erupted in the stock market. Not just for any stock, but for virtually anything with a techy sounding name. Valuations, when available at all, went through the roof, as did stock prices for a time. We know now that this excess was grossly fueled by the stimulative practices of the U.S. Fed, but it sure felt good at the time.

The first years of the twenty-first century undid all that. Paper fortunes made were lost. Yesterday's hottest company became today's casualty. Investment geniuses fell back to earth gracelessly. It is against this backdrop that a wave of Chinese fortunes were made from the country's export strength. Chinese exporters with dollars to spare might have considered stocks very seriously. But what did they see? They saw the market whipsawing other investors back and forth. Frightened, many would turn their attention to the perceived security of real estate.

At the time of this writing, the U.S. housing market after crashing has been flat on its back for several years. Meanwhile, the burgeoning Chinese economy shows no sign of letting up. Deep in the background of noise from Capitol Hill are calls for China to do something about its mind-boggling stash of American dollars. As it happens, the United States is one of the few countries in the world to permit non-citizens to purchase real estate. Anyone with any knowledge about the Chinese mindset could have predicted what would happen next.

The Chinese seen arriving by the thousands at American airports do not just have tourism on their mind. These are not the poor immigrants of earlier eras seeking a place to rest their heads. Indeed, these latter-day arrivals probably don't seek to stay in the United States at all. But they do have one thing on their mind, property.

Consider the mindset of these purchasers. Despite China's opening, many restrictions remain on the purchase of real estate in that country. Even if real estate prices were compelling, the bureaucratic red tape involved with its purchase would dissuade many. Compared with Chinese red tape, the process of purchasing property within the United States is amusingly simple. Meanwhile, the dollars earned from China's torrent of exports sit impatiently idle. What to do with them becomes immediately apparent.

Just as the landowner in olden times saw immovable land as the surest store of value, so do modern Chinese investors. Other investment vehicles like stocks and bonds have their merits but are too remote and intangible for most new investors. Owning even a relatively large number of shares of Microsoft, for instance, would not permit anyone to call the company one's own. That's not the case with real estate properties.

According to the National Association of Realtors, investors from China taking advantage of low housing prices in the United States were estimated to have made nearly 10 percent of all sales for the year ending March 2011. This percentage is especially staggering when one considers that Chinese investors have been active in other developed countries as well.

If American political history is any guide, this will undoubtedly lead to politicians calling for China to curb its excess. The critics will likely focus on how the Chinese are taking housing away from Americans while forgetting that it is Chinese purchases that are keeping house prices from falling even further. But there is no stopping the trend. From New York to Honolulu, from London to Sydney, Chinese buyers are swooping in to purchase prime real estate. It remains for us to grasp the lesson.

FOR THE LONG TERM ONLY

Two very important caveats are in order. First, notwithstanding what the Chinese or anyone else is doing, it must be stated that the primary reason ordinary folks should consider buying real estate is for a place to live. If only for the experience to be gained in the process of home purchasing, people must make their home their first real estate purchase, preferably one in which to live for a long time. Overseas investors might not live in their owned American properties, but domestic investors must.

Sounds obvious enough, right? Well, unfortunately, the point was not obvious enough for the many, many people in recent years who chose to participate in a practice known as *flipping*. These people had no intention of ever occupying their purchased property. Nor did they plan to hold it as an *investment*. Rather, they made it their practice to buy with the sole purpose of reselling it very shortly thereafter.

For a few years, this practice of flipping proved highly lucrative. Experienced flippers made quite a game of buying as much property as they could afford and immediately selling it. This game made enough sense when the property markets were headed straight up, with no obvious signs of slowing down (are there ever any obvious signs?). In such frothy markets, flipped properties could be reflipped sequentially for subsequent gains. For a time, flippers had some justification to think themselves geniuses.

But all parties must end sometime. The spiked punch at this particular party was the combination of exceptionally low interest rates and curiously lax lending standards at banking institutions. When, for a variety of reasons, the punch bowl was taken away, so were the opportunities to flip properties. Flippers, not accustomed to property prices falling or even holding steady, were caught very off-guard. Stretched as they were to buy their properties, flippers were left holding unsellable properties, with heavy mortgages to boot.

The wreckage left in their wake will take years to repair. My point is, don't let that happen to you. Don't treat what will likely be your single largest investment as a game. Buy it primarily as a hospitable place to raise your family. Let its investment potential be a big side benefit.

The second caveat concerns liquidity. Real estate will ultimately be more valuable than cash in the bank but is nowhere near as accessible. This is called *liquidity*, the ability to turn something into cash. For obvious reasons, cash in the bank is as liquid as any investment can get. In contrast, except during the hottest markets, real estate is just about as illiquid an investment as the average person will ever see. However, real estate's illiquidity is not at all a problem if the buyer genuinely purchased the property as a place to live.

This second caveat reinforces the first. One leaves cash in the bank for the possibility of needing it on a moment's notice. Your home, however, is not a vehicle that you could easily liquidate if a need arises. Therefore, as exciting as it sounds to invest in real estate, it should only be done with money that won't be needed anytime soon.

FIRST AND FOREMOST

In one of my favorite movies of all time, *Superman*, Lex Luthor, played by Gene Hackman, declares that "stocks may rise and fall, utilities and transportation systems may collapse . . . but (people) will always need land." That pretty much sums it up. We can debate the merits of the movie, but this one line, uttered by a fictitious character, is incontrovertible and directly to my point. Combining Lex Luthor's accurate observation about people always needing land with Mark Twain's accurate observation that they're not making it anymore explains in a nutshell why everyone must consider owning real estate.

The Chinese are far from alone in appreciating this intuitively. The first great appeal of purchasing property is its sheer tangibility. What's so real about real estate is that it can be seen, touched, and trampled upon. There's nothing to not understand about a house on a plot of land or even raw land. It might not be pretty. It might be downright ugly. But there's nothing mystifying about real estate. You buy it, you own it, you do what you want with it, including sell it.

The same cannot be said for even the most basic financial products, such as stocks and bonds. Can just anyone understand what he or she is getting when buying a share of stock in a corporation? For that matter, does everyone even know what a corporation is? I don't think so. Believe me—it takes the entirety of my first lecture to get these points across in my college finance courses. After explaining it, I believe some students might even be dissuaded from owning stocks. That's not bad. People who truly cannot understand the mechanics of stocks should not own them.

Consider how daunting the task is for a new investor just starting out. The person reads the financial magazines or watches the business press and becomes intrigued about the chance to make money. So the person gathers up his or her financial resources and with the courage of Jason and the Argonauts ventures forth to conquer and invest. Now what? If the person is like most everyone else, he or she will see the innumerable stock listings along with the many, many professional opinions and will feel very daunted very quickly. Whom to believe? After all, this one says buy a particular stock, and that one says sell it. How to judge who's right? One might as well throw darts. (For years, the *Wall Street Journal* ran monthly contests comparing stock picks from professionals with stocks selected by monkeys throwing darts at the stock listings. The monkeys won frighteningly often.) Just as in any other field, there will undoubtedly be a small number of people who'll turn out to be prodigies, and I hope you are one of them. But far more people venturing into the market will come away disillusioned.

However, I believe that everyone who's even moderately financially solvent should seriously consider owning real estate. It all boils down to this. Although there are very few people who can accurately assess stocks and stock markets, almost anyone can obtain a sense of the condition of his or her intended neighborhood. Don't believe me? Try asking 10 diligent amateurs—or if you have access to them, professional forecasters—for their thoughts about the prospects of a particular company 10 years from now. I'd be willing to wager that you'd obtain 10 highly varying forecasts.

But try that same experiment with 10 ordinary people who live in a particular community and ask their opinion about the neighborhood's property values in 10 years. This time I'd wager that you'd find a consensus. Why is this the case? Because the variables that will affect the prices of stocks are literally innumerable. So wide reaching are the variables that even most professionals must subspecialize into specific areas of expertise. How then should we expect 10 of them to agree when in all likelihood they're analyzing different variables?

In contrast, the number of variables that affect any particular community is relatively small. Even if the amateurs cannot specifically delineate them, their opinions will be drawn from commonsense observation. What are the amenities of the community? What is the quality of schools? What about crime in the area? How good is access to transportation? These are issues that do not concern just you or me or the 10 amateurs. They interest everyone everywhere who purchases a home.

THE ROOF OVER YOUR HEAD

It bears stating the obvious that having a roof over our heads is just about our most primal need, behind only food and oxygen. That, of course, is a good enough reason to own a piece of real estate. But most people won't be satisfied with just this. And they shouldn't be when there are tremendous gains to be made in the long term from owning property. Think of the beauty of it. Is there anything else that you can use thoroughly until you're done with it and still sell for a gain later? Isn't this as close as we can come to having our cake and eating it too?

Economists and real estate appraisers might quibble about exactly how it's done, but in general, real estate can be counted upon to grow with its locality's economy. This shouldn't be too surprising. If county A experiences tremendous economic growth for whatever reason, it stands to reason that homes in county A will appreciate as people move in to take advantage of those opportunities. (Remember Lex Luthor's comment.) After all, economic gains don't occur in a vacuum. They come from the innovation, entrepreneurship, and diligence of people. And these people need a place to live.

Necessarily, regional growth is spread unevenly across a country as vast as ours. Consider a charming little city named

Redmond, Washington, before mighty Microsoft moved in. Redmond was probably a nice place to live before Microsoft, but consider the boost to the local economy when the start-up grew to dominate an entire industry. What necessarily happens to home prices of residents in Redmond? After all, one can safely assume that Microsoft employees will want a home in the area. After years of "using" their homes, they can cash in those homes for much, much more than they'd paid originally. Try doing that with a car. To lesser degrees than in Redmond, this same process is replicated all across the country over the long term. For anyone, but especially for a people who have a deep attachment to their families and estates, this is a major appeal of owning real estate.

THE MAGIC OF MORTGAGES

Most people in the United States probably do not have a full appreciation of the wonderful depth of our mortgage market. Yes, I know some people will have trouble believing this, especially while the financial crisis is still being unwound. Yes, I am fully aware of the difficulties that everyone had during the crisis in obtaining credit. But let's put this in perspective. The proper comparison is not our banking system in its current condition versus the system in its prime. It should be our banking system versus those of other countries in the world. During more normal times, I believe any objective assessment of our financial system would conclude that it has provided remarkable opportunities for people to buy real estate.

Notwithstanding the faults and flaws of banks, government regulators, and entities such as Freddie Mac and Fannie Mae in recent years, the American banking system is still driven to a large extent toward providing people credit for the purchase of homes. Indeed, some of the big financial problems we've faced in this country were due to banks not sticking to their knitting. But when they do, as indeed they did for generations, banks provide genuine firepower for the American dream.

Let's start by defining the key terms. What is a mortgage? Most technically, a mortgage is actually not the loan made for the purchase of real estate. More accurately, that is known as the *mortgage loan*. The term *mortgage* by itself refers to the means by which the lender holds a stake in the property that was purchased with the loan. This may seem a trivial distinction, but it underlies the difference between mortgage loans and personal or credit card loans.

For those latter two types of loans as well as for student loans, the only assurance that the bank will receive its money back is the good faith of the borrower. In an unfortunate number of cases, that is like having no assurance at all. Of course, the bank has legal means to pursue repayment from the borrower, but no banker ever wishes to go down that path. The matter from the bank's perspective would get resolved a great deal easier if it had something of value of the borrower's to sell in the event of the borrower's failure to repay. This is called *collateral*.

Almost anything can be offered as collateral, but it is the bank's responsibility to adjudge it properly. Not just anything that belongs to the borrower will cut it. Most should not. Agriculture can rot. Automobiles can be driven away. Boats can sail. But the collateral that gladdens the heart of any banker the most is something valuable and immovable—like real estate. With real estate purchases, in exchange for the loan from a bank to purchase the real estate, the borrower gives a mortgage to the bank on that same property. This mortgage is said to encumber the property until the loan is fully repaid to the bank. A mortgage is the use of real estate for collateral, plain and simple. The bank doesn't own the property during this time. The bank doesn't own it until and unless the borrower completely defaults on repayment of the loan, at which point the nightmarish rigmarole of foreclosure commences. Most people are aware of the many frightening stories about bank foreclosures during the economic crisis.

It is easy to see why banks like making mortgage loans. People who owe money on a mortgage loan will do just about anything in their power to repay it rather than lose their shelter. This makes mortgage loans rather secure forms of credit in normal times. But if repayment is not made, the bank has a second avenue of repayment in the form of property foreclosure, which is taking the mortgaged property from the borrower. This provides a high degree of insurance to the bank. The immovability of real estate makes it much, much easier to claim than attempting to repossess someone's car, for instance. As a result, for generations, the primary activity of most local and even large banks was quite understandably the making of mortgage loans.

It is even easier to see why consumers like mortgage loans. First of all, everyone likes credit of any sort. But for what is probably the largest purchase anyone will make in a lifetime, there is little chance for the average person to earn enough in his or her early years to make such a purchase outright. Mortgage loans thereby enable the enjoyment of home ownership for the many by fast-forwarding the purchase by decades.

The ability of American consumers to so relatively easily obtain mortgage loans has been an undeniable strength of our economy for generations. Even before the Internet made banking entirely ubiquitous, consumers, even those with bad credit, even those who were not American, had many avenues available when buying American real estate. This has not been the case in most other countries and is not the case now in China. The eventual recovery of the American banking system would once again make our mortgage market the envy of the world.

THE NUTS AND BOLTS OF MORTGAGES

This book cannot do justice to the full range of detail involved in obtaining a mortgage loan. There are more specific books to do that. However, this section can at least provide a basic introduction.

So you've located a home to purchase. Perhaps you canvassed 10 amateurs and wound up agreeing with each one of them. You think the price is acceptable. Like most everyone else, you don't have enough cash in the bank to purchase it outright, and so you wish to borrow the lion's share of the purchase price. What next?

The most important mortgage terms with which you must be familiar are *principal, interest rate, amortization*, and *term to maturity*. When you get deep into comparing offerings from different banks, all are moving parts, and so keeping definitions straight is absolutely necessary.

The first one is simple. The principal is simply the amount of money you are borrowing. Anyone who can do basic arithmetic can come up with this number. Take the home price plus the attendant costs of buying the home and subtract how much you wish to pay out of your own pocket. That's it. The number left is the principal amount of the mortgage loan you seek.

Interest gets a little tougher, but not much. We just need a little math beyond arithmetic. I think most people appreciate that lenders don't lend for free. How they get paid is not by charging a flat dollar amount but instead by charging a certain percentage of the amount lent. That's easy enough to understand. If the interest rate on a $100 loan is 10 percent, then the borrower pays $10.00 on the loan for every year that the $100 is outstanding.

What makes it slightly confusing is that when borrowing money, whether for a mortgage or a student loan or a credit card loan, one usually sees two numbers quoted as a percentage. One is called the *rate*, and the other is the *yield*. Which is more important to you? The answer is that the second number is more important, although you wouldn't think so from common advertisements. The first number is called the *annual percentage rate*, the *APR*. The yield is the *annual percentage yield*, the *APY*. They are very similar in name but very different in usage.

The critical difference between the two is the hypercritical concept of compounding, which we encountered in Chapter 5 from the savings perspective. The point is identical but from the opposite direction when applied to mortgage loans. To reiterate the main point from Chapter 5, compound interest arises when interest is charged on the principal amount and then on the interest previously earned. The formulas are as follows:

$$\text{APR} = \text{periodic rate} \times \text{number of periods in a year}$$
$$\text{APY} = [(1 + \text{periodic rate})^{\text{number of periods in a year}}] - 1$$

Notice that the number of periods in a year is merely multiplied by the periodic rate in the APR calculation. However, for APY, 1 + the periodic rate is then raised to the power of the number of periods in a year. Let's see how the numbers differ.

For example, let's say the bank charges 1 percent interest per month. If so, the APR would be simply the 1 percent times the number of months in a year, or 12 percent.

However, this does not take into account the compounding of interest during the course of the year. When this is done, you'll find that the APY is actually 12.68 percent per year, 0.68 percent higher than the APR.

The APR as a borrowing rate is only truly accurate if you borrow money on the first day of the month, pay it off on the last day of the month, and borrow the same amount on the first day of the next month. If you did that, each month you would pay the monthly rate of 1 percent, which actually does add up to only 12 percent per year. But obviously, doing this would be unwieldy and highly unrealistic.

You will find that the APR or the APY will be made more obvious depending on whether you're borrowing or investing money. Since the APY will always be higher than the APR, if you were investing money, which would you think the bank will be quicker to disclose? Obviously, to attract your money, it would quote the APY.

But the opposite is true when you're borrowing money from the bank. In that case, the bank has an incentive to quote the lower (though still true) rate to attract your business. Therefore, for mortgages, the more commonly stated interest rate is the APR simply because it is lower and therefore more attractive to the borrower. But in truth, it is the APY that is more important to you, the borrower.

The third term to understand is *amortization*. To amortize something is to whittle it away over time. That something is the *principal amount*. It gets whittled away by the monthly payments you make to the lender. That amount is called the *amortization*. Sounds simple enough, right? But unfortunately, we need yet a little more math to address it.

Why isn't the amount just called the repayment? The answer is that no conventional mortgage permits one to pay all the principal back in one lump sum. Instead, all lenders require some little piece of the principal to be repaid along with the monthly interest payment. This is harder to figure than it sounds. Even most professionals require a financial calculator to do this. The reason is that most borrowers would like the stability of making the same dollar amount of payment each month. But this doesn't seem to jibe if some principal is being reduced every month. Amortization strikes the balance. It is the precise dollar amount that, when paid every month through the term of the loan, reduces some principal each month while maintaining the APY. Got that? Don't even try to do this by hand. Just use a financial calculator.

Let's assume that you have borrowed $300,000 at 6 percent per year for 30 years. The amount of monthly mortgage payment you'd need to make is $1,798.65. You would find that if you diligently paid $1,798.65 every month for 30 years, you would precisely have paid 6 percent per year on your money while amortizing your principal by just enough that on the very last month of the thirtieth year, you would have fully repaid the debt. A truncated version of the rather complicated illustration is shown in Table 7-1.

The last term to understand is *term to maturity*. How long do you want to borrow the money for? The concept is simple enough, but the application can get involved. If

TABLE 7-1

MONTH	MORTGAAGE PAYMENT, $	INTEREST CHARGED, $	PRINCIPAL REPAID, $	REMAINING PRINCIPAL, $
1	1,798.65	1,500.00	298.65	299,701.35
2	1,798.65	1,498.51	300.14	299,401.20
3	1,798.65	1,497.01	301.65	299,099.56
4	1,798.65	1,495.50	303.15	298,796.40
5	1,798.65	1,493.98	304.67	298,491.73
6	1,798.65	1,492.46	306.19	298,185.54
7	1,798.65	1,490.93	307.72	297,877.82
8	1,798.65	1,489.39	309.26	297,568.56
9	1,798.65	1,487.84	310.81	297,257.75
10	1,798.65	1,486.29	312.36	296,945.38
11	1,798.65	1,484.73	313.92	296,631.46
12	1,798.65	1,483.16	315.49	296,315.96
13	1,798.65	1,481.58	317.07	295,998.89
14	1,798.65	1,479.99	318.66	295,680.24
15	1,798.65	1,478.40	320.25	295,359.99
16	1,798.65	1,476.80	321.85	295,038.13
17	1,798.65	1,475.19	323.46	294,714.67
18	1,798.65	1,473.57	325.08	294,389.59
19	1,798.65	1,471.95	326.70	294,062.89
20	1,798.65	1,470.31	328.34	293,734.55
21	1,798.65	1,468.67	329.98	293,404.58
22	1,798.65	1,467.02	331.63	293,072.95
23	1,798.65	1,465.36	333.29	292,739.66
24	1,798.65	1,463.70	334.95	292,404.71
Years 3 through 29 omitted from this illustration				

(continued)

TABLE 7-1 *(Continued)*

MONTH	MORTGAAGE PAYMENT, $	INTEREST CHARGED, $	PRINCIPAL REPAID, $	REMAINING PRINCIPAL, $
349	1,798.65	104.49	1,694.16	19,204.25
350	1,798.65	96.02	1,702.63	17,501.62
351	1,798.65	87.51	1,711.14	15,790.48
352	1,798.65	78.95	1,719.70	14,070.78
353	1,798.65	70.35	1,728.30	12,342.48
354	1,798.65	61.71	1,736.94	10,605.54
355	1,798.65	53.03	1,745.62	8,859.92
356	1,798.65	44.30	1,754.35	7,105.57
357	1,798.65	35.53	1,763.12	5,342.44
358	1,798.65	26.71	1,771.94	3,570.50
359	1,798.65	17.85	1,780.80	1,789.70
360	1,798.65	8.95	1,789.70	(0.00)

you simply asked people how long they wish to borrow your money for, they might answer, for as long as possible. Now ask them the same question if they must pay interest on it. This time they might answer, for as short a time as possible. Then ask them the same question after you've illustrated the case with amortization examples. For instance, compare the monthly payments of the $300,000 mortgage loan at 6 percent for 15 versus 30 years.

We just saw that for 30 years, the payment would be $1,798.65. For the same mortgage at 15 years, the payment jumps to $2,531.57. You'll see that the monthly amortization payment for a 30-year loan is considerably lower than for a 15-year loan. So you might choose the longer term. But that is only until you consider the total amount of interest you would have paid out over the course of the 30 years.

This math is easy enough to calculate with the full benefit of the spreadsheet illustration we just saw in truncated form. Take my word for it that the total interest charged for the 30-year loan is an eye-popping $347,514.57. In contrast, the total interest charged over 15 years is a considerably less eye-popping amount of $155,682.69, a difference of $191,832.88.

Now you may reverse your opinion and find that the shorter loan is preferable after all. As you can see, the question you must answer is not so clear. The applicable interest yield is given to you by the market. You will not have any say other than yes to this bank or no to that bank. You will also not have any say on the amortization because it is determined entirely by the math. After the buyer has decided on the principal amount, the deceptively simple issue of term becomes the single most important issue for the buyer to address.

GIFTS FROM UNCLE SAM

It is said that the only certainties in life are death and taxes. There's unfortunately no escaping the former, but the latter can be managed. Even better, one doesn't need a high-priced tax accountant to access these gifts from Uncle Sam. It's a bittersweet benefit actually. One can only derive tax savings because one is taxed in the first place. The greater the savings, the greater must be your tax rate. But it works in reverse too.

The greater your tax rate, the greater the benefits of tax savings. Therefore, the greater your tax rate, the greater should be your incentive to own a home. There are two major tax benefits of home ownership.

1. In its incredible beneficence, the IRS permits the interest paid on a mortgage loan to be deducted from one's taxable income. No other form of loan has such a generous benefit these days. As a result, mortgage rates, already low by historical standards at the time of this writing, are effectively lower still. Someone in the 35 percent tax bracket holding a mortgage loan with an APY of 5 percent would actually be paying 3.25 percent. The formula for this is simply:

   Actual mortgage cost = mortgage rate × (1 − your tax rate)

2. Further in its beneficence, the IRS gives a wonderful tax break upon the eventual sale of your primary residence. At the time of this writing and for the foreseeable future, homeowners can make a gain of $250,000 (or $500,000 for married couples) from the sale of their home and not pay tax on it. Not even a capital gains tax. That alone, for many people, can be a primary tipping point between owning and renting a home. It's almost like free money from the government. No other investment can match that kind of gift from the IRS.

A GREAT LEAP FORWARD

For many Chinese, owning one's own home is merely the first step toward their real estate dreams. Like the tasting of a tempting delicacy, once one's appetite has been whetted, there is no doing without more. The initial home purchase is just that delicacy. Many people rather quickly move to subsequent real estate purchases, not usually for a personal residence but for the investment potential. For many Chinese, their appetite for real estate may even exceed their enormous appetite for cuisine.

This brings us to the topic of property investing. What exactly is it? Strictly speaking, buying your home is already an investment. After living in your home for years, its value will presumably increase, probably greatly. Unlike a stock or other financial investment, one cannot easily sell it for its value during its rise. But with deliberate planning, many people can substantially fund their retirements with a carefully planned sale of their home. What's more, current tax laws permit the aforementioned $250,000 or $500,000 gains from the sale of a primary home to be untaxed.

Beyond the investment in your home, there are great opportunities to be made from real estate investing elsewhere. In fact, some of the world's vastest fortunes have been made from investing in real estate. Donald Trump comes immediately to mind. But believe it or not, fortunes much greater than his have been made in the Far East from investment property. To the average American, the names Li Ka-Shing, Cheng Yu-tung, and Lee Shau Kee may be unfamiliar. However, each of these people has become a multibillionaire the old-fashioned Chinese way, via property investment.

I do not assume that the reader of this book will have the opportunity to pursue multimillion dollar properties like these tycoons did. But in general, the risks that a more prosaic investor would face are similar. Not everyone will have the appetite for these risks, but dreams of millions of dollars drive those who do.

THE CASH FLOW METRIC

Ongoing cash flows are the name of the game in regular property investing. The presumed long-term payoff from the sale of the property, great as it might be, is actually a rather small part of the consideration. There's no denying that one should expect a gain on the eventual sale of the property. But there'll be a lot of water under the bridge before that distant time. And in that time lies the great virtue of property investing.

What do people do with property that they don't need to occupy? They rent it out for someone else to occupy. That's it in a nutshell. Notwithstanding the great benefits of owning your own home, there will always be a great mass of people who have neither the inclination nor the ability to buy a home. The reasons why are unending. And property investors are grateful for them because they are the "clients" of property investors.

The cash flow calculation takes account of the entire stream of rental income and compares it with all the costs of buying and maintaining the property. Sound simple? It is. No matter how elevated you may wish to take the analysis, it gets conceptually no harder than this:

Cash inflows – cash outflows = free cash flow

However, and it's a big however, the simplicity of this concept masks a world of complexity (and possibly tears) in its implementation.

Let's consider the outflows first. The biggest outflow by far is actually the least interesting. That would be the monthly payment on the mortgage loan you took out to buy the property. It's the least interesting because for most people (and even for most professional property investors), the loan will be a plain vanilla, fixed-rate loan. The beauty of it is its unvarying nature. You will know from day one exactly how much you must pay per month for the life of the loan. This makes it quite easy to project forward. I doubt even a novice would ignore this biggest and most important outflow.

But as they say, the Devil can be found in the details. And the profitability of a real estate investment is crucially contingent on the details of cash outflows. There are three primary considerations after the mortgage payment that can break an otherwise fine property deal.

First is the property tax. Your mortgage payment may be fixed, but property taxes will not be. Even the most diligent of investors cannot know what the future property tax assessments will be. But some conservative estimation is mandatory. The taxes will not stay where they are. In fact, the weakened financial condition of most municipalities strongly suggests that taxes will rise considerably. You can never be too precise here, and so tailor in some conservatism in your forecasts.

Second is property insurance. Everything said above about imprecision in estimating property taxes also goes for insurance. There should be no skimping on property insurance. Just as with health insurance, not having it just that one catastrophic time you need it could destroy you financially.

Third is maintenance costs. This one at least gives you some wiggle room. Like any physical thing, a piece of real estate requires upkeep and regular maintenance. Do you have the willingness to reinvest money to maintain the property? If not, at least you have an alternative. It's called *sweat equity*. If you don't wish to pay someone else to do it, you can choose to do it yourself.

Now let's consider the inflows. Here is where the beauty of property investing comes alive. What are the inflows? That one seems easy enough. It's how much you can charge the tenant for renting the property. There will definitely be times when a property sits unrented, thereby generating no income at all. But in more normal times, property investing provides an excellent hedge against rising inflation. Why? Because as inflation rises, you, the landlord, have the eventual opportunity to raise the tenants' rents!

Remember that although property taxes, insurance, and maintenance costs will also rise, the biggie, the mortgage payment, will not. This is the great appeal of real estate investing for the patient long-term investor. It is in the later years when the cash flow metric takes off with a vengeance, especially after the mortgage itself is fully paid off.

SUMMARY

Those of us lucky enough to live in the United States may sometimes underestimate the wealth of possibilities available in real estate. But to the Chinese, there is no underestimation. The vastness of our country combined with the wealth of financing opportunities makes the United States a veritable buffet of choices for the conscientious investor. The recent turmoil in the financial markets and its effect on property values should not dissuade people from the long-term picture. At a minimum, the ownership of a piece of property for one's primary residence provides an excellent start to this manner of investment. From there, depending on one's motivation, the sky's the limit. And we have our seventh principle of the Chinese Way to Wealth and Prosperity.

CHAPTER EIGHT

DO NOT
AS THE
CHINESE DO

All the previous chapters in this book had the explicit goal of helping readers achieve prosperity by elucidating traits that the Chinese people have used to obtain theirs. These are positive examples that use illustrations intended to spur imitation. On the other hand, there are negative examples, examples of what not to emulate. For instance, in Chapter 4, I had used the U.S. government as a negative example of how to handle debt.

In this chapter, tragically, it is necessary to make an example of a less favorable trait of the Chinese. One negative trait above all has bedeviled the Chinese people for generations. It is the insidious disease of gambling. There are few things more destructive of wealth than the inclination and compulsion to play games of chance. Regrettably, it is the vice of choice in every Chinese community in the world.

There is surprisingly little stigma against gambling in the Chinese community. Women are as avid gamblers as men, and even the elderly partake in the frolic. I had one friend in grade school who ran bets to the local OTB after school with the full consent of his parents. I have even known deeply religious Chinese Christians (including said friend) who feel no compunction about hitting the casinos. Where there should be shame, there is acceptance. It is a disgraceful blemish on the otherwise shining Chinese record of achievement.

THE CHINESE GAMBLING SCENE

Crowds start forming rather early each morning in New York City's Chinatowns (there are more than one now) for the buses that will take them to the casinos. You see the travelers congregating before nondescript storefronts from which the tickets are sold, gripping plastic bags full of pastries and oranges to consume during the three-hour trip south to Atlantic City or north to the Foxwoods and Mohegan Sun resorts. It's usually a quiet crowd that gets unruly only once, and then only slightly, as jostling commences upon boarding. Entire families show up together, and one could be forgiven for thinking the buses were taking them on a shopping excursion to the mall. They're not going to a mall, but for many Chinese, a trip to the casino is as typical as a trip to the mall is for the average American family.

When Americans go to casinos, it is usually for the rush of excitement similar to what children experience upon entering Disney World. In contrast, especially for working-class Chinese, the freneticism of casinos is a welcome relief from the even greater freneticism of their daily lives. For these Chinese, a trip via the casino express is a combination of a scenic tour and a culinary excursion in addition to a relaxing vacation. The casinos cater to this. They know they're not just in the gambling business anymore. That may be their big moneymaker, but they're in the hospitality business as well, and they know just who butters their bread.

But the casinos can't be held primarily to blame. They're just the most opulent venues of the Chinese propinquity to gamble. Venture into any Chinatown in the world and listen carefully. Make your way into the basement hovels that often function as makeshift community centers. Before long, you'll hear the strident clattering of mahjong tiles. It is the same game played around card tables in Florida retiree communities. However, there's a big difference. The chips or tokens being wagered may well represent someone's entire net worth.

When I was a boy, my father would frequently take me to such places, where I'd greet one uncle or another. My father was not himself much of a gambler, but it was clear from the intensity of voices and demeanors that most of the other men were. These were not the elite gamblers who are showered with freebies and preferential treatment at the luxury casinos. These were rather poor folk who couldn't have had much more than a few hundred dollars to their name. But the odious stench of cigarettes and hard liquor in the basements could not mask the stench of desperation emanating from the men. These were hardened gamblers, but most must have known that they'd end the day or night broke.

Several decades later, I was touring San Francisco where my sister had moved. On the tour bus mocked up to look like a trolley car, the driver was pointing out the sights of the city as we passed them. We got to a park in Chinatown, and he noted several elderly men playing Chinese checkers. Charming he said. Then he added that on a typical day over a million dollars in bets changed hands at those lonely park tables. I didn't check his facts. But I didn't doubt them.

According to Jesse Brown Cook, who served the San Francisco Police Department from the late 1880s to the 1930s, as early as 1889, there were already 62 lottery agents, 50 fan-tan games, and 8 lottery drawings in San Francisco's Chinatown. And that was long before gambling was legalized. We're talking about a serious cultural obsession. Steps are not being taken to prevent it.

A STATELY PLEASURE DOME

Ask people at random to guess what city has the world's biggest gambling market, and you'd most likely hear them guess Las Vegas. If you told them that this answer is wrong, they might follow up with Atlantic City. Or perhaps Monte Carlo. All would be wrong. In fact, the world's largest gambling market is in the tiny Chinese enclave of Macau, with a population of less than half a million people. Remarkably, despite such a tiny population, Macau's gambling revenue is a whopping four times larger than that of Las Vegas.

It is also here that the world's richest gaming tycoon resides. No, it's not Donald Trump or Sheldon Adelson or Steve Wynn. It's Stanley Ho, a name very likely unfamiliar to most Westerners. However, in the Far East, it is his name that is virtually synonymous with gambling.

Stanley Ho is known as the king of gambling because for 40 years, he held the monopoly on gambling in Macau. His position was never challenged because he carefully cultivated his relationship with the Portuguese who controlled Macau for centuries. In time, this multibillionaire would extend his holdings beyond Macau to China, Portugal, Vietnam, the Philippines, Mozambique, East Timor, and even North Korea.

But his ascent commenced in improbable Macau. It would be difficult to imagine a less likely locale to find the world's most thriving gambling market. For much of recent history, Macau functioned as a trading port for the Portuguese, but a far inferior one to neighboring Hong Kong. There was nothing to particularly distinguish Macau. Tourist attractions were pedestrian; cuisine was uninspired; people were identical to those you'd meet in Hong Kong. My first and only visit to Macau during my college years unearthed nothing to inspire a return visit. In fact, I wanted out after only half a day.

But that all changed in 2002 when the Macau government announced an end to Stanley Ho's gambling monopoly. All hell broke loose as one gambling palace after another opened its doors. All the biggies came to town: Sands, Wynn, Galaxy, MGM. Like in the fictitious field of dreams, the overriding feeling was that if we build it, they will come. Sure enough they did. Miraculously, just five years later, Macau overtook the Las Vegas Strip in gambling revenues. Now Macau has fully 33 casinos, with the crown jewel being the Venetian Macau.

If Macau never provided any compelling reason to visit for much of its past, its present has more than compensated for this past shortcoming. The Venetian alone has 550,000 square feet of casino space with 3,400 slot machines and 800 gambling tables. In addition, the Venetian provides its guests with a 15,000-seat arena, 3,000 suites, and 1,200,000 square feet of convention space. There are probably entire cities that could rest comfortably within the Venetian's confines.

It doesn't take much imagination to envision some tycoon wanting to wrest away the Venetian's crown as the world's largest casino. Real estate competition is as common in Asia as popularity contests are in American high schools. The new champion is probably only a few years away in development. And all the competitors will get to share in the spoils of even more fevered gambling.

Anyone who hasn't seen Macau in recent years would not recognize it now. It isn't that gambling is new. Even before Mr. Ho gained monopoly rights, gambling had been permitted in Macau since 1851. But until 2002, this wasn't the glitzy world of Vegas and Monte Carlo gambling. It was more like the grown-up cousin of the basement gambling joints that haunt the world's Chinatowns, smoky, seedy, and very disreputable. Criminal activity, which always seems to haunt casinos, operated remarkably openly. But all that displeased the territory's masters in Beijing.

There hasn't exactly been a crackdown as much as a stare-down by the authorities. I doubt the authorities would mind wiping out the criminal gangs that infest Chinese society, but there is another consideration foremost in their minds, money. Crackdowns are bad for business.

There's no wrestling this horse back into the barn, and there's certainly no one interested enough to take on the role of the wrestler. Gambling tourism is now Macau's biggest source of revenue, making up 50 percent of the economy. That's a larger percentage of the Macau economy than military spending is of the U.S. economy.

And who's providing all this revenue? Not surprisingly, the answer is visitors from China who require a visa just to visit this Chinese city. Tour junkets arriving from China are as common as vacationers to Orlando. Macau, which wasn't always so easy to get to, now has a modern airport to accommodate these arrivals, bypassing Hong Kong's sparkling new one.

The problem is that prying Chinese away from their cherished gambling is one tough job. Official admonishment against gambling has had no effect. What's more, the authorities themselves seem to be a part of the problem. They are great customers of the casinos they ostensibly should be policing.

According to Zeng Zhonglu, a professor at Macao Polytechnic Institute, government officials reported losing an average of $2.7 million each. I can't imagine what kind of government official would admit to this sort of thing, but there you go. Moreover, a 2008 study of high rollers from mainland China showed that one-third were government officials. Now, how exactly can a government official have the stakes to be a high roller? It stands to reason that to fuel their gambling habit, some have pillaged state funds. In fact, new authorities have become necessary to police the authorities because the corruption has gone so far. Many of the worst have been sent to prison, and at least 15 have been executed for their crimes. These are the most extreme examples of the cost of gambling addiction, but far from the only ones.

THE HUMAN COST

In America, the pernicious disease of gambling affects more than 15 million people. Of these, over 2 million meet the criteria for pathological gambling, the worst form. It is characterized by an urge to gamble despite harmful consequences or a desire to stop. Although the American Psychological Association classifies pathological gambling not as an addiction but as an impulse control disorder, that's only so much semantic quibbling. It has all the hallmarks of addiction, like those for drugs, alcohol, or food.

Like drug addicts, gambling addicts can't control their impulse to gamble, even though they are fully aware of how much their habit is hurting them and their families. Also as with drug addicts, gambling is all they can think about even when they're not actually engaged in gambling. They'll keep gambling despite all warnings and despite everything they stand to lose. They just can't stay away.

According to Sam Skolnik, author of *High Stakes: The Rising Cost of America's Gambling Addiction*, America's gambling addiction isn't too far behind the nation's drug problem. He reports that in 2007, Americans lost more than $92 billion gambling, about 9 times what they lost in 1982 and almost 10 times more than what moviegoers in the United States spent on tickets that same year. In his book *Gambling in America*, Baylor University professor Earl Grinols estimates that addicted gamblers cost the United States between $32.4 billion and $53.8 billion a year—about $274 per adult annually.

That's bad enough, but it gets worse. A 1995 survey by Gamblers Anonymous found that 56 percent admitted to some illegal act to obtain money to gamble. The survey reported that 58 percent admitted they wrote bad checks, while 44 percent said they stole or embezzled money from their employer to feed their habit. Such stark statistics should make some citizens and politicians think twice before voting to let a casino enter their jurisdictions.

THE MEDICAL MANIFESTATION

Gambling addiction is now a recognized mental health problem. It may not be a crime, but there are victims nevertheless. The victims begin with the addicts themselves.

Medical experts report that although more men than women suffer from pathological gambling, women are developing the disorder at higher rates. Even more worryingly, the disorder deepens in women at a faster rate than in men. The experts have determined that while men tend to become addicted to more interpersonal forms of gaming, like blackjack, craps, or poker, women tend to engage in less interpersonally based betting, like slot machines or bingo. With a propensity to engage in such forms of impersonal betting, women do not even have the stigma of losing in public as a possible deterrent.

On the very day I wrote these words, the news reported about the suicide of a woman in Vancouver who suffered from gambling addiction. She had accumulated $150,000 in gambling debts, which she could not pay off. Apparently, she recognized the extent of her malady and enrolled in a self-exclusion program that requested casinos to prohibit her entry. But it was all too late. She was already addicted, and the financial cost had accrued. She raised the total cost to the ultimate level.

Let's be clear about this: gambling addiction is a severe medical condition. It is not just a desire to gamble or even a compulsion to. It is a physical inability to stop. The gambling addict can no more stop wanting to gamble than he or she can fly. There is increasing scientific evidence that this is so.

One culprit seems to be the chemical dopamine. A theory holds that this brain chemical is triggered by the thrill and excitement of gambling and even by the ambience of the casino. The release of dopamine fuels the gambler's addiction further. According to the American Medical Association, up to 10 percent of people who originally took dopamine for Parkinson's subsequently developed a gambling addiction.

Another culprit is the chemical serotonin, which is also related to clinical depression. Individuals who have a low level of serotonin in the brain have been found to be at higher risk for developing pathological gambling, possibly as a by-product of depression. But even if not directly related to depression, deficiencies in serotonin are known contribute to compulsive behavior, such as compulsive gambling.

A third possible medical culprit is the chemical norepinephrine. According to the Illinois Institute for Addiction Recovery, recent evidence indicates that pathological gambling is an addiction similar to chemical addiction. It has been seen that some pathological gamblers have lower levels of norepinephrine, which is secreted under stress or arousal, and so pathological gamblers gamble to make up for their deficit.

The final result is very similar to a drug addiction. The potential for monetary reward in gambling produces brain activation very similar to that of a drug addict receiving cocaine.

Tragically, the poor woman in Vancouver is not unique. The National Council on Problem Gambling reports that one in five pathological gamblers attempts suicide, a rate higher than for any other addictive disorder. Although other addictions also have a bottom-line cost, that for gambling seems to be greatest, for understandable reasons.

GAMBLERS ANONYMOUS

Something must be done. The impact on wealth creation aside, something must be done for humanitarian reasons. Problem gambling has been shown to be a cause of dysfunctional families as well as the aforementioned rates of suicide and attempted suicide.

Fortunately, there is an active intervention program for gambling addicts modeled on Alcoholics Anonymous. Gamblers Anonymous uses the 12-step program that was originated by Alcoholics Anonymous and that has been borrowed for other support groups as well. These 12 steps are: We

1. Admitted we were powerless over gambling—that our lives had become unmanageable.

2. Came to believe that a Power greater than ourselves could restore us to a normal way of thinking and living.

3. Made a decision to turn our will and our lives over to the care of this Power of our own understanding.

4. Made a searching and fearless moral and financial inventory of ourselves.

5. Admitted to ourselves and to another human being the exact nature of our wrongs.

6. Were entirely ready to have these defects of character removed.

7. Humbly asked God (of our understanding) to remove our shortcomings.

8. Made a list of all persons we had harmed and became willing to make amends to them all.

9. Made direct amends to such people wherever possible, except when to do so would injure them or others.

10. Continued to take personal inventory and when we were wrong, promptly admitted it.

11. Sought through prayer and meditation to improve our conscious contact with God, as we understood Him, praying only for the knowledge of His will for us and the power to carry that out.

12. Having made an effort to practice these principles in all our affairs, we tried to carry this message to other compulsive gamblers.

Successful participants in 12-step programs for any addiction attribute their improvement to the strength of the community of others in the same boat. This seems minor, but those afflicted with the disease of gambling probably can't conceive of anyone being able to help them out of their crisis. They are wrong. Many have been helped before, and many remain to be helped by the humanitarians of Gamblers Anonymous.

THE OPPORTUNITY COST

It may also help to put to the pathological gamblers the actual-dollars-and-cents cost of their addiction. It is possible that these individuals might never have seen the ledger of their lost money. Even if they do know, they may not fully appreciate the eventual accumulated cost of those lost wagers.

In finance and economics, there is a critical concept known as *opportunity cost*. It refers to the opportunities that are forgone because time and resources are directed in another arena. Money lost on gambling has a very great opportunity cost. Our previous chapter about the power of compound interest can be used to illustrate this. How much future wealth has been destroyed by the gambler's indulgence in his or her fancy? The greater the indulgence, the greater this destruction.

I believe if the unfortunate addicts could see in black-and-white terms how much money they are forgoing for their retirement, they would sooner realize the financial tragedy they are creating for themselves.

SUMMARY

It truly pained me to include this chapter. However, I would be very remiss not to. Gambling is indeed rampant in the Chinese community. But this is not the sport of kings. Gambling is a great barrier to prosperity. Gambling is a tax. Beyond taxing the addicts' finances, gambling taxes the very soul of the least fortunate. It is a crisis that our community must do more to combat. It is a tragic lesson, but it is an important one to share for anyone interested in obtaining wealth.

Epilogue

This book had its genesis in a conversation I had with Eric Tyson, the author of many personal finance titles in the For Dummies line of books. At the time, the global economy was on its back, the national mood was down in the dumps, and the publishing industry was immeasurably challenged, but Eric encouraged me to write this book.

At first, I didn't think it could fly. I thought that a book about getting rich quickly might win approval, but a book about getting rich slowly, which in the final analysis is what this book is about, surely could not. But fortunately I was wrong.

Fortunately also, America has a place for any new opinion. The free-for-all that is American discourse is wonderful for welcoming initiates to the table. The authors of our Bill of Rights would be very pleased.

In regard to economics, there is much occasion these days to exercise our freedom of speech. So let's join in. There has been talk of an end to America as the world's superpower. However, such talk is not entirely new. A generation ago, there was similar talk. We were warned about the consequences of a national malaise, a crisis of confidence. We feared the economic ascendance of Japan as many fear of

China now. We worried that ours would be the last generation that could automatically expect a higher standard of living than our parents had. Does all this sound familiar?

But after talking, we must act. We must act as the people and entrepreneurs of the United States did in disproving the doomsayers a generation ago. Those who held to their bearishness about America were proved ridiculously wrong, as under Presidents Reagan, Bush (H. W.), and Clinton, the United States experienced the greatest economic expansion in the country's history.

In my introduction, I emphasized that the traits of the Chinese people I detail in this book are very valuable aspects of human capital that warrant emulation. But I also made clear that these principles are not unique to the Chinese people. One group of people who would certainly have known all these principles very well were America's earliest settlers. There was nothing they didn't know about prudence, fiscal or otherwise. And they bequeathed us the most fertile setting that history has ever seen for prosperity to grow.

I therefore have supreme confidence in America's future. No amount of bumbling by political mediocrities can offset the full force of America's entrepreneurial spirit. When this powerful spirit is combined with an accommodating free market, the most productive force known in economics is unleashed.

If we would incorporate the lessons that the Chinese can provide and that I believe the Puritans and Pilgrims would have endorsed, America will remain the shining city on a hill that John Winthrop envisioned when he arrived on these shores.

Index

MICHAEL JUSTIN LEE was born in Hong Kong and raised in New York City's Chinatown. Previously Professorial Lecturer at Georgetown University and Practitioner Instructor at Johns Hopkins University, he is currently on the faculty of finance at the University of Maryland, where he is a past University Senator.

Professor Lee completed his undergraduate degree in East Asian studies at Brown University and received his graduate education at Andover-Newton Theological School and New York University, graduating Beta Gamma Sigma with an MBA in finance from the latter institution. A veteran Chartered Financial Analyst, in 2003 he was appointed to serve in the administration of U.S. Secretary of Labor Elaine Chao as Financial Markets Expert-in-Residence.